# CONTENTS

Search by theme:

Or search by topic:

Audience
Clarity
Credibility
Decision-making
Feedback
Image
Message
Preparation

using the grid overleaf.

# BUSINESS COMMUNICATION ESSENTIALS

| | Audience | Clarity | Credibility | Decision-making | Feedback | Image | Message | Preparation | PAGE |
|---|---|---|---|---|---|---|---|---|---|
| **Q1** Why is effective communication important? | | ☑ | ☑ | ☑ | | ☑ | ☑ | | 2 |
| **Q2** Why is clarity essential for effective communication? | | ☑ | | | | | | | 4 |
| **Q3** How does being an effective communicator affect my personal credibility and professionalism? | | | ☑ | | | | | | 6 |
| **Q4** How might my communication style affect business relationships? | ☑ | ☑ | ☑ | ☑ | | ☑ | ☑ | | 7 |
| **Q5** What questions should I ask before I communicate? | | | | | | | | ☑ | 9 |
| **Q6** Where does the communication process start? | ☑ | | | | | | ☑ | | 11 |
| **Q7** Once I have a 'message', what follows? | ☑ | | | | | | ☑ | | 12 |
| **Q8** After the message and the coding, what else can I control? | ☑ | | | | | | ☑ | | 13 |
| **Q9** After I have transmitted my message, what happens next? | ☑ | | | | | | ☑ | | 15 |
| **Q10** What are the key barriers to communication? | | ☑ | | | | | | | 17 |
| **Q11** How can I minimise the barriers to communication? | | ☑ | | | | | | ☑ | 21 |
| **Q12** How can I help people retain my message? | ☑ | | | | | | ☑ | ☑ | 23 |
| **Q13** Why is listening important? | | | | | ☑ | | | | 24 |

| BUSINESS COMMUNICATION ESSENTIALS | Audience | Clarity | Credibility | Decision-making | Feedback | Image | Message | Preparation | PAGE |
|---|---|---|---|---|---|---|---|---|---|
| **Q14** Why should I ask for feedback? | | | | | ☑ | | | | 25 |
| **Q15** How should I use feedback? | | | | | ☑ | | | | 26 |
| **Q16** Why is preparation key to communication? | | | | | | | | ☑ | 27 |
| **Q17** When communicating, what should be my primary focus? | ☑ | | | | | | | | 28 |

| BUSINESS COMMUNICATION TECHNIQUES | Audience | Clarity | Credibility | Decision-making | Feedback | Image | Message | Preparation | PAGE |
|---|---|---|---|---|---|---|---|---|---|
| **Q18** How important is it for me to be able to articulate my purpose? | | ☑ | | | | | | ☑ | 30 |
| **Q19** What should I learn about my audience? | ☑ | | | | | | | | 32 |
| **Q20** How important are my choice of words, facts or analogies? | | | | | | | ☑ | | 34 |
| **Q21** Is there an ideal way to deliver a message? | | | | | | | ☑ | | 35 |
| **Q22** Is there an ideal way to deliver bad news? | | | | | | | ☑ | | 36 |
| **Q23** How best can I deliver unsettling messages? | | | | | | | ☑ | | 37 |

| BUSINESS COMMUNICATION TECHNIQUES | Audience | Clarity | Credibility | Decision-making | Feedback | Image | Message | Preparation | PAGE |
|---|---|---|---|---|---|---|---|---|---|
| **Q24** How much information should I include? | | | | | | | | ☑ | 38 |
| **Q25** How much background information should I provide? | | | | | | | | ☑ | 39 |
| **Q26** Why should I avoid speaking *ad lib*? | | | | | | | ☑ | ☑ | 41 |
| **Q27** How should I order my thoughts? | | | | | | | ☑ | ☑ | 42 |
| **Q28** What should I consider when I use images? | ☑ | ☑ | | | | | ☑ | ☑ | 45 |
| **Q29** How should I factor location and timing into my communication? | ☑ | | | | | | ☑ | ☑ | 47 |
| **Q30** How can I prepare for an emotional audience? | ☑ | | | | | | ☑ | ☑ | 49 |
| **Q31** Why is it important to anticipate objections? | | | | ☑ | | | | ☑ | 51 |
| **Q32** Why does being empathetic matter? | | | | ☑ | | | | | 52 |
| **Q33** What's the risk in over-generalising? | | | | | | | ☑ | | 54 |
| **Q34** Why are analogies useful? | ☑ | ☑ | | | | | ☑ | | 55 |
| **Q35** Why is it important to fact-check? | | | | | | | | ☑ | 56 |
| **Q36** How serious is violating confidentiality? | | | ☑ | | | | | | 57 |
| **Q37** How can I use my hands and my facial expression to enhance communication? | | | | | | | ☑ | | 58 |

| MEETINGS & INTERVIEWS | Audience | Clarity | Credibility | Decision-making | Feedback | Image | Message | Preparation | PAGE |
|---|---|---|---|---|---|---|---|---|---|
| **Q48** How can I get the best from a formal meeting? | | | | | | | | ☑ | 78 |
| **Q49** How should I prepare for a formal meeting? | | | | | | | | ☑ | 80 |
| **Q50** Why do I need a written agenda for a meeting? | | | | | | | | ☑ | 83 |
| **Q51** How important is the length and timing of a meeting? | ☑ | | | | | | | ☑ | 85 |
| **Q52** As chairperson, how should I manage a meeting? | | | | ☑ | | | | | 86 |
| **Q53** As chairperson, how can I encourage participation at meetings? | ☑ | | | | ☑ | | | | 88 |
| **Q54** Why should I prepare minutes of a meeting? | | | | ☑ | ☑ | | | | 90 |
| **Q55** How should I prepare to interview a candidate for a position in my organisation? | | | | | | | | ☑ | 91 |
| **Q56** How can I improve as a recruitment interviewer? | | | | ☑ | | | | | 92 |
| **Q57** Should I prepare questions or just chat with a candidate? | | | | | | | | ☑ | 94 |
| **Q58** How should I prepare for a job interview myself? | | | | | | | | ☑ | 95 |
| **Q59** What questions should I ask if I am a candidate for a position? | | | | | | | | ☑ | 98 |
| **Q60** What kind of personal examples should I offer in a job interview? | | | ☑ | | | | | | 99 |

| MEETINGS & INTERVIEWS | Audience | Clarity | Credibility | Decision-making | Feedback | Image | Message | Preparation | PAGE |
|---|---|---|---|---|---|---|---|---|---|
| **Q61** What if something goes wrong with a meeting? | | | ☑ | ☑ | | | | | 100 |
| **Q62** What are my responsibilities as chairperson of a formal meeting? | ☑ | | | ☑ | | | | | 101 |

| WRITING – OFFLINE & ONLINE | Audience | Clarity | Credibility | Decision-making | Feedback | Image | Message | Preparation | PAGE |
|---|---|---|---|---|---|---|---|---|---|
| **Q63** What types of writing do I need to master? | ☑ | ☑ | | | | | | | 104 |
| **Q64** Why is time important when writing? | | ☑ | | | | | | | 105 |
| **Q65** How does the written word differ from the spoken word? | | ☑ | | | | | | | 106 |
| **Q66** Why do I need to think about specific readers when writing? | ☑ | | | | | | | ☑ | 107 |
| **Q67** What should I look for when I reread my work? | | ☑ | | | ☑ | | | | 108 |
| **Q68** What are the basic formats of memos and letters? | | ☑ | | | | | | | 110 |
| **Q69** How is writing an email different from writing a letter or memo? | | ☑ | | | | | | | 112 |

| WRITING – OFFLINE & ONLINE | Audience | Clarity | Credibility | Decision-making | Feedback | Image | Message | Preparation | PAGE |
|---|---|---|---|---|---|---|---|---|---|
| **Q70** What should I include in the minutes of meetings? | | | | ☑ | ☑ | | | | 113 |
| **Q71** How should I structure a formal report? | | ☑ | | | | | | | 114 |
| **Q72** What makes a good title for a report? | | ☑ | | | | | | | 116 |
| **Q73** How can I help my reader understand complex material? | | ☑ | | | | | | | 117 |
| **Q74** Can I put my opinions in a report? | | ☑ | | | | | | | 119 |
| **Q75** What is the difference between a recommendation and a conclusion? | | ☑ | | | | | | | 121 |
| **Q76** What should I consider when developing visuals? | | | | | | | | ☑ | 123 |
| **Q77** Why are titles essential for charts and graphs? | | ☑ | | | | | | | 124 |
| **Q78** How can I make a slide more effective? | | ☑ | | | | | | | 125 |
| **Q79** How should I use charts and visuals in a report? | | ☑ | | | | | | | 127 |
| **Q80** How should I acknowledge other people's contribution to a report? | ☑ | | ☑ | | | | | | 129 |
| **Q81** What must I beware of when using social media for my organisation? | | | | | ☑ | | ☑ | | 130 |

| SPEAKING & PRESENTING | Audience | Clarity | Credibility | Decision-making | Feedback | Image | Message | Preparation | PAGE |
|---|---|---|---|---|---|---|---|---|---|
| **Q82** What should I look for when I visit the venue in advance of my talk? | | | | | | | | ☑ | 132 |
| **Q83** What should I wear when making a presentation? | | | | | | | | ☑ | 134 |
| **Q84** How important is practising my presentation? | | | | | | | | ☑ | 136 |
| **Q85** Should I use notes during my presentation? | | | | | | | ☑ | ☑ | 138 |
| **Q86** Should I provide the audience with handouts? | ☑ | | | | | | ☑ | ☑ | 140 |
| **Q87** How can I be interesting if I have given my talk before? | ☑ | | | | | | | ☑ | 142 |
| **Q88** Why is making eye contact with the audience important? | ☑ | | | | | | | | 143 |
| **Q89** Must I include visuals in a talk? | | ☑ | | | | | | | 145 |
| **Q90** How should I introduce my visuals? | | ☑ | | | | | | | 147 |
| **Q91** How can I help my audience retain information? | ☑ | | | | | | ☑ | ☑ | 148 |
| **Q92** Should I practise with my visuals? | | | | | | | | ☑ | 149 |
| **Q93** How can I prepare to answer questions? | | | | | | | | ☑ | 151 |
| **Q94** How can I stop being so nervous before a presentation? | | | | | | | | ☑ | 153 |
| **Q95** How should I handle team presentations? | | | | | | | | ☑ | 155 |

| SPEAKING & PRESENTING | Audience | Clarity | Credibillity | Decision-making | Feedback | Image | Message | Preparation | PAGE |
|---|---|---|---|---|---|---|---|---|---|
| **Q96** How can I use sound or video in my presentation? | | ☑ | | | | | ☑ | ☑ | 157 |

| ACHIEVING BUSINESS COMMUNICATION EXCELLENCE | Audience | Clarity | Credibillity | Decision-making | Feedback | Image | Message | Preparation | PAGE |
|---|---|---|---|---|---|---|---|---|---|
| **Q97** How can I improve my ability as a communicator? | ☑ | ☑ | | | ☑ | | | | 160 |
| **Q98** What should I seek to learn from other speakers? | | | | | ☑ | | | | 162 |
| **Q99** How can I develop my writing skills? | | | | | ☑ | | | | 164 |
| **Q100** To continue to improve as a communicator, what kind of feedback should I look for? | | | | | ☑ | | | | 165 |

# BUSINESS COMMUNICATION ESSENTIALS

# Q1    Why is effective communication important?

Most of us take the process of communicating for granted. For good reason, after all, we have been doing it throughout our lives: at home, in a shop, on the bus, in the airport, in the office or at school.

But, although we communicate all the time, we don't always do so successfully. We know this to be true because of the frequency with which we hear or use phrases like: "What did you mean by...?", "But I thought you said ...", or "Could you clarify that last point?". Each of these phrases suggests miscommunication, always an undesirable situation.

Consider the following scenario:

> On Wednesday, Frank promises Pauline that he will have Gary send her a copy of a confidential report. It includes data for her presentation on Friday. However, Frank forgets to tell Gary to give the report to her.
>
> What happens?
>
> When Pauline doesn't receive the report, she calls Frank or Gary to ask for it. If she contacts Frank first, he may say that he is sorry, that he'll send it along promptly. If she contacts Gary first, he may not have a clue as to what she is talking about. Not having spoken to Frank, Gary may not be sure whether Pauline's request for a confidential document is legitimate. So now what? Phone calls, texts or email may ensue: from Gary to Frank, from Gary to Pauline, from Frank to Pauline. Priorities change. Work is stopped or interrupted — all because of a minor failure to communicate. Gary is annoyed and embarrassed. Pauline is frustrated, under pressure and angry. Frank feels guilty. In the meantime, Pauline's work is delayed; she's counting on the data in the report.

Scenarios like these happen all the time. We are human and make mistakes. Imagine if each one of us failed to communicate accurately with only one of our many colleagues just once a day. Multiply those slip-ups by thousands of interactions. The potential for disruption could be staggering.

Think about your own experiences:

- Ever had to read a memo or email twice because you couldn't make sense of it on the first reading?
- Ever had to read a memo or email out loud in an effort to understand it?
- Ever had to phone colleagues to see if they understood what was said at a meeting?
- Ever received a follow-up email written to clarify an earlier one?
- Ever had to attend an impromptu meeting called to explain the information that was distributed in a memo?

If you answered 'yes' to any of these, then you know that miscommunication is wasteful. Miscommunication makes people feel unsure, angry, confused, embarrassed, disgusted, frustrated or humiliated. That's just the human cost — there may be other consequences too if the wrong materials are ordered, work is delivered to the wrong customer, incorrect prices are charged and so on.

Better communication might avoid these problems. Rather than spending time clarifying, apologising, chasing missing reports, or making unnecessary phone calls, you can focus on what you had planned to do. More careful communication uses your resources more effectively.

**See also**

Q2    Why is clarity essential for effective communication?
Q3    How does being an effective communicator affect my personal
      credibility and professionalism?
Q4    How might my communication style affect business relationships?
Q5    What questions should I ask before I communicate?
Q11   How can I minimise the barriers to communication?
Q17   When communicating, what should be my primary focus?
Q97   How can I improve my ability as a communicator?

## Q2    Why is clarity essential for effective communication?

To be successful as a communicator, you need to be clear.

Selling – a key role in business – involves convincing others of the value of your products or services. Annual reports, inter-office memos, texts, faxes, email, watercooler chats and staff meetings are all opportunities to persuade also.

As a manager, you are often in a position to influence some kind of change. For instance, when you:

- Counsel an employee about lateness, you are encouraging that person to alter their behaviour;
- Make a presentation to prospective clients, you are convincing them that your organisation can meet their needs;
- Write a progress report, you are informing others about what transpired over a period of time and explaining why specific actions were appropriate.

Therefore, it's important that what you communicate is clear.

The more precise you are, the more accurate you are, the more likely it is that your audience will understand what you intended and will be able to act on your message. They also will feel more secure, knowing that what they are doing is what you expect them to do. The employee will be on time; the client will work with you, and your audience will accept your rationale.

Clarity enables you and others to do your jobs without unnecessary questioning, anxiety or second-guessing. Rather than having to restate your ideas three or four times to make your point, seek to express your ideas clearly the first time.

**See also**
**Q1**    Why is effective communication important?

**Q3**    How does being an effective communicator affect my personal credibility and professionalism?

**Q4**    How might my communication style affect business relationships?

**Q18**    How important is it for me to be able to articulate my purpose?

## Q3    How does being an effective communicator affect my personal credibility and professionalism?

By being accurate, thoughtful, clear, and prepared, good communicators save resources, enable others to understand their responsibilities, make and influence decisions – and thus they appear credible and professional.

Have you ever had a supervisor ask you to work on a project without giving you a clear idea about what was expected of you? When your brief is clear, you know where to begin; when you know the purpose and the parameters of your assignment, you know what to do; when the goal is explicit, you know when you have done your job.

It's not only projects that can bewilder. How many times have your eyes rolled as you have said a silent, "Oh, no, not again" as you are summoned to an impromptu, agenda-less meeting run by someone who allows the discussion to meander through tangential issues when you have an urgent phone call to make or report to finish by a deadline?

People are grateful to managers who are thoughtful communicators, who plan and think through issues; those managers are respected for their sensitivity to other people's commitments. When you think about your colleagues, which of them do you consider to be the most professional? Why? Does their communication style affect your opinion?

The people we admire are usually good listeners, they speak and write clearly, they ask insightful questions and they run meetings well. What they share is typically thoughtful, polished, organised, and to the point. They are credible and professional and so we respect them. You should aim to be respected in this way too.

### See also
Q2     Why is clarity essential for effective communication?
Q4     How might my communication style affect business relationships?
Q18    How important is it for me to be able to articulate my purpose?
Q97    How can I improve my ability as a communicator?

## Q4 How might my communication style affect business relationships?

It is a given that business involves relationships – be they with clients, colleagues, customers, employees, shareholders, or subcontractors. And with the exception of the problematic employee, who despite supervision is still unwilling or unable to take direction, or the unsatisfactory subcontractor you want to replace, you want to establish and maintain these relationships over the long-term. An effective and sensitive communicator can do just that, while an ineffective or insensitive one may do damage.

Being aware and being sensitive means knowing how, when and why you communicate what you do and understanding the implications of your choices. Are you patient or abrupt? Terse or long-winded? Pleasant or patronising? Do you acknowledge people or ignore them? Are you gracious or rude?

Whenever you have an interaction with another person or group of people, ask yourself what you are trying to accomplish. Are you trying to win over a new client? Influence an old one? Train a new employee? Advise a senior partner? Assuage a disgruntled customer? Or hope someone will leave without your asking?

And you know there are consequences to treating people well or treating them thoughtlessly. For example, how might you feel if:

- You had been made to wait for 20 minutes, even though you had arrived on time for a meeting?
- You had to speak to someone who gave you the sense that you were interrupting a private conversation?
- You made a suggestion, and no one acknowledged or reacted to your idea?
- Your colleague ended a phone call with a click rather than a good-bye?

- You were made to stand, when everyone else in the room is offered a chair?
- You were told to expect a call by day's end, and none came.

How you communicate can make people feel important or unimportant. You can make people feel good or bad. You can make people feel demeaned or respected.

And remember that people share their experiences. Unhappy customers share their unhappiness with other customers. Frustrated clients tell other clients about their anger or disappointment. Rejected candidates associate their experiences with your products or services. Disaffected employees complain to each other. Disgusted purchasers may shop elsewhere. In contrast, while research shows that positive experiences also are shared, fewer positive experiences are shared than negative ones.

Therefore, whether you are making a phone call, writing a letter, memo, or email, having a face-to-face conversation, or not responding at all, think about how your communication style affects the relationships that you currently have and those that you want to have. Whether you are reporting to your boss, addressing the board, speaking to a secretary or handyman, consider the consequences of your communication style.

Recall interactions you have had with clients or colleagues. Consider how their communication styles affected your working relationships.

**See also**

| | |
|---|---|
| **Q3** | How does being an effective communicator affect my personal credibility and professionalism? |
| **Q10** | What are the key barriers to communication? |
| **Q17** | When communicating, what should be my primary focus? |
| **Q46** | In a high-speed electronic world, is there time for courtesies? |
| **Q97** | How can I improve my ability as a communicator? |

## Q5     What questions should I ask before I communicate?

Before you communicate, take the time to make informed decisions. While it may only take you a few moments to do so, too often we act first and think later. Get into the habit of asking yourself some basic questions even before a simple one-on-one discussion.

The questions to ask yourself are Kipling's 'six honest servingmen' – the tried and true Who, What, Why, When, How and Where:

- **Who?** Ask yourself with whom you are communicating. Who is your audience? Knowing the demographics of that audience helps you to determine the best way to share your message. When it is pertinent, find out the age, sex, education, nationality, job title and/or the relationship of the audience to you and to any other people present. Knowing about your audience helps you decide on your words, approaches or analogies. Will you be insulting their intelligence by explaining too much or speaking over their heads if you don't? Will you be using language that they don't know or discussing issues with which they are already familiar?

- **What?** Ask yourself what information you want to give out. Then, decide how much information is sufficient to make the point you want to make. Determine what background to the material or details you need to provide to ensure understanding;

- **Why?** Ask yourself why you are sharing what you are saying, drawing or writing. Decide on your motivation. Has an incident prompted a change of plan or policy? Are you anticipating concerns because additional staff are being hired? Have there been staff problems because people are adjusting to a new approach to supervision? Are you encouraging or rewarding entrepreneurial thinking? Are you counselling someone who has been away ill?

- **When?** Check the time of day, the day of the week or the time of the year to decide how the timing might affect what you are saying. Is it the end of a quarter, when people are under pressure to achieve sales targets or to finalise paperwork? Is it the day before a holiday weekend or a key meeting? People react differently at different times;

- **How?** Ask yourself how you should share what you want to communicate. Decide which method is best for the given situation and the individuals involved. Is speed important? Is face-to-face or voice-to-voice contact essential? Is thorough documentation demanded? Is distance a factor? Time zones?

- **Where?** Is a chat outside the office on neutral turf the best approach or would a formal meeting in-house be better?

Effective communicators reflect on the situation and make appropriate decisions before they communicate.

**See also**
Q4      How might my communication style affect business relationships?
Q6      Where does the communication process start?
Q10     What are the key barriers to communication?
Q17     When communicating, what should be my primary focus?

## Q6 Where does the communication process start?

Using the theory behind the communication process, you can examine your daily interactions objectively. Doing so is one of the best ways of improving your communication abilities.

The theory describes how the exchange of ideas works in abstract terms, what actually transpires when we communicate.

The process begins with a message that you want to transmit to your audience. Hopefully that audience receives it, reacts to it and gives you feedback. That response may then lead to another message, then another and so on.

What is a 'message'? It is a thought, an idea, a feeling or notion. So, the first step in the process is to have a message you want to share with someone else. A message can be:

- **Simple:** "Hello" or "Good to see you";
- **Straightforward:** A warning to 'mind the gap' on the Underground or not to forget your umbrella;
- **Complex:** A series of recommendations for restructuring your business;
- **Brief:** Just a few words in a tweet;
- **Lengthy:** A 250-page report or a 30-minute speech.

In essence, whatever you want to share with one, two or many people is your message – and that's where your communication process starts.

**See also**
Q7 Once I have a 'message', what follows?
Q8 After the message and the coding, what else can I control?
Q9 After I have transmitted my message, what happens next?
Q10 What are the key barriers to communication?

# Q7     Once I have a 'message', what follows?

Communication theory indicates that we begin with a message that we want to share and then that we encode that notion.

Encoding covers a wealth of choices. You can use words, written or spoken. You can paint a picture, make a movie, or choreograph a ballet. You can use gestures. You can give a thumbs up or down. You can pull faces. You can draw pictures. You must decide what will best convey your ideas.

In business, we send messages all the time to colleagues in our own or other offices, across town or across the ocean. Whether you are sending them over the radio or *via* satellite into a living room, you make choices about whether words, gestures, symbols or images would be best. You decide whether written words, spoken words or photographic images would make the point in a presentation. Your choices need to fit the situations – for example:

- Would you draw pictures, use spoken language or hand gestures to assist a 787 land at an airport?

- Would you use words, images or gestures to conduct an orchestra and to make the musicians change tempo?

- Would you use words, images or gestures to praise or reprimand a subordinate?

- Would you use words, images or gestures to convince a new client of the effectiveness of your organisation?

You decide. You choose.

### See also
Q6     Where does the communication process start?
Q8     After the message and the coding, what else can I control?
Q9     After I have transmitted my message, what happens next?
Q10    What are the key barriers to communication?

## Q8 After the message and the coding, what else can I control?

Communication theory helps us see what we control. We decide the message, we decide the 'code' and, as the developer of the message, then we decide how to send or transmit it to the audience.

And in business, you have many options for sending your message to your audience – including:

- Giving a speech to a group;
- Sending an email;
- Distributing a report through inter-office mail;
- Sending a fax;
- Making a phone call;
- Posting a letter;
- Hanging a motivational sign on the wall;
- Texting a thought;
- Tweeting a reaction;
- Photographing an image;
- Sketching a blueprint;
- Waving a greeting;
- Winking an acknowledgement;
- Smiling a greeting;
- Frowning in dismay;
- Giving a colleague a 'high five';
- Chatting in the corridor; or
- Designing a model.

Each of these represents a way of sending a message to your audience. The choice is in the hands of the person with the message – you. So you must decide on the most effective method of transmission.

**See also**

**Q6**    Where does the communication process start?
**Q7**    Once I have a 'message', what follows?
**Q9**    After I have transmitted my message, what happens next?
**Q10**   What are the key barriers to communication?

# Q9 After I have transmitted my message, what happens next?

You have a message, and you know how you want to encode it and send it to your audience. Up to this point, you are in charge of the process. You, the person with the idea, make all the decisions.

However, once the message leaves your lips, or you hit the send button or put some writing into an inter-office envelope, your control of the process is over for the moment.

Control now shifts to your audience. If they have received your message – whether it is literally on their minds or in their hands – they, not you, have the opportunity to decode it, interpret and react to what you have transmitted.

But, first, they must receive it, decode it and interpret it: only then can they react.

Their reaction to your message is your feedback, and it can take many forms. Suppose you choose to:

- Tell a joke – your audience may or may not laugh;
- Provide written recommendations to your clients – they may accept or reject them;
- Propose a new policy to the board – the directors may or may not approve it;
- Make a sales pitch – your customers may or may not buy;
- Draw a picture – your audience may misunderstand or misinterpret it.

As the sender, you no longer have control of the process. You cannot control what the receiver of your message does.

All you can do is to listen, look for and weigh the reactions you receive and try to determine what they mean. Perhaps the audience didn't understand your meaning. Maybe your frame of reference wasn't clear.

In addition, pay attention to any questions you are asked. Are they on one specific aspect or on several areas of what you said or wrote? Do people seem confused by your message? Did you receive a memo asking for clarification? Did you get no reaction whatsoever?

Whatever responses you get, recognise them as feedback and learn from them. Perhaps your report was too long, too short, too vague, too detailed or just right. Your talk was off-target or tangential. Your counselling session was misunderstood. Whatever your message, expect feedback.

But, if you get no reaction whatsoever, check to make sure that what you sent was actually received. Silence due to non-receipt is different from silence as feedback!

**See also**

**Q6**    Where does the communication process start?
**Q7**    Once I have a 'message', what follows?
**Q8**    After the message and the coding, what else can I control?
**Q10**  What are the key barriers to communication?

## Q10 What are the key barriers to communication?

Barriers to communication include:

- Lack of clarity;
- Word and image choices;
- Choice of medium;
- Physical barriers.

### Lack of clarity

You want to be sure that others receive your message exactly as you sent it. You want it to arrive in the hands or ears or eyes intact. In essence, you want your message to be understood.

The easiest way to block communication is to 'waffle' or be vague. Can you recall politicians you have heard or instructors you have had on training courses whom you couldn't understand because they used unfamiliar terms or indecipherable abstractions? Have you ever read books or listened to speeches that fit those categories? Perhaps you wondered why you were unable to grasp the concept. Most likely the problem wasn't with you at all; it was due to the speaker's, instructor's or writer's inability to communicate their ideas clearly.

Corporate mission statements provide prime illustrations of unclear language. Such statements usually include wonderful words like 'vision', 'trust' and 'responsibility'. Unfortunately, many are written in such high-flown language and convoluted sentence structures that they have little or no meaning for the people involved in the day-to-day operation of an organisation – one of the constituencies for which these statements are designed.

Think about how easy it is to confuse, cause anxiety or foster second-guessing simply by being unclear.

## Word and image choices

Quite simply, you can lose or confuse your audience by selecting imprecise, inaccurate or inappropriate words or images for a given situation. You need to take a few moments to think about the ones you are using. Consider these three sentences:

- "It would appear that we have some concerns with regard to the budget";
- "We need to weigh the implications of what transpired";
- "It is important that we follow through on those kinds of issues".

Do you understand what was intended by the speaker? What are the 'concerns' in the budget? What aspect of the budget is causing the concern? What are the 'implications'? What 'has transpired'? What 'kinds of issues'? What kind of 'follow through' is important? Too often, communicators make incorrect assumptions about what other people understand.

The same may be true with your choice of images. A blurred photograph, a graph with no title, or an image that enchanted you but had no connection to your ideas, simply serves to confuse.

## Choice of medium

As a communicator, you must decide which method of communication is most effective for whatever you plan to share. Remember you can write, you can speak, you can sign, or you can paint. And, if you write, you may opt to text, email or distribute a memo, or write a short or long report. If you choose to speak, is it face-to-face? By phone? In a group meeting? On line? On air? But given the myriad of choices, it is easy to make the wrong one.

You need to assess the message and determine the best method for getting that message to your audience. In fact, you may block your message by selecting the wrong communication medium. What follows are some absurd notions, which nonetheless make the point:

- Would you expect airport ground crews to send faxes to a pilot taxiing a plane down the runway?

- Would you ask your secretary to type all your urgent phone messages and give them to you at the end of the week?
- Would you call a staff meeting at the end of January to express condolences to a colleague who had lost a loved one in early December?
- Would you send a memo to staff announcing a fire in the conference room?
- Would you email an employee to tell him/her that he/she has been made redundant? (Some people do, sadly!)
- Would you send a letter by slow post to a client overseas indicating that there is a dangerous design flaw in your product?

Good communicators are sensitive to the nuances of diverse audiences and channels, and they make educated decisions about what is most appropriate in a given situation and with the individuals involved.

### Physical barriers
Physical barriers may prevent your idea from reaching its intended audience:

- You may not be heard because you speak too softly;
- Faxes may be blurred or have missing pages;
- Email may not be read because the address is typed incorrectly or unknown, the system is 'down', or the recipient gets over 1,000 emails a day so he or she barely has time to read the important ones and deletes the others;
- Voice mailboxes may be full, messages may not be recorded, or may be deleted too quickly;
- Notes may be lost in a pile of papers on a desk;
- Reports may be distributed to the wrong offices;
- Construction noise in the room next door may prevent you from hearing what was said in your own office or may interfere with a talk you are giving;

- Mobile phones may ring, despite repeated requests that they be turned off or put in silent mode.

**Other barriers**

In addition, you can block communication if you 'turn off' your audience. It is easy to do this inadvertently. And if the audience takes offence at some small part of your message, they may dismiss the rest of it. Worse, they may choose to dismiss or diminish the importance of future messages.

You can alienate your audience by patronising them, by demeaning them, or by treating them as if they weren't intelligent or experienced enough to understand or value what you have to say.

You also may create a barrier between you and your audience by:

- Avoiding eye contact;
- Sitting while they stand;
- Forgetting names;
- Failing to share information or to follow through as you promised;
- Lying;
- Being inattentive;
- Appearing arrogant;
- Being poorly groomed;
- Telling an inside or inappropriate joke or anecdote;
- Being – or appearing – unprepared.

**See also**

Q2     Why is clarity essential for effective communication?
Q4     How might my communication style affect business relationships?
Q11    How can I minimise the barriers to communication?
Q17    When communicating, what should be my primary focus?
Q20    How important are my choice of words, facts or analogies?

## Q11 How can I minimise the barriers to communication?

To enable your message to get through to your audience, take some time to anticipate as many potential barriers as you can. In other words, consider what might interfere with your efforts to get your message across.

Might you encounter contextual issues or people problems? Does the audience know or need to know the background, or are there personality issues or group dynamics issues that might arise? Is a particular individual under unusual stress because of a re-organisation or because of some serious personal problems, or is the organisation going through an audit, and is someone worried about being laid off?

Even if the barriers you face are not that dramatic, you should:

- **Know yourself:** Are there aspects of your personal style that create problems? Do you have a booming voice? Do you whisper? Do you avoid eye-contact and appear aloof? Do you have a tendency to mumble? Do you stutter under pressure?

- **Know your office:** Do you share space and have little privacy? Are your responses delayed because you and your phone lines are overloaded? Are your colleagues and/or assistants polite? Is the importance of good customer service engrained? Are you short-handed?

- **Know your equipment:** Are reports delayed because of the endless queue at the photocopier? Is your printer slow? Can the equipment handle the volume of material that you or your office produces?

- **Know the organisation:** Are there political problems? Have some of your colleagues been bypassed for promotion and now are bitter or angry? Is a union dispute distracting people? Is there a big contract in the offing that has everyone on tenterhooks? Are you dealing with a number of new hires on a learning curve?

- **Know the calendar:** Is it the Friday before a long holiday weekend? Is it a dreary Monday following a holiday break? Are there always staff meetings on certain days? Are the Christmas holidays over and are people stressed about money and the short and dark days?

- **Know people:** Are you communicating with a new, angry or frustrated client? Or (hopefully) a satisfied client? Are you communicating with people who are tired, resentful or demotivated? Or are they always optimistic, or driven or ambitious? Have you little time to communicate your message?

This kind of quick, conscious analysis takes only a few minutes of reflection. Determine those aspects of work that may create barriers and then think about the best way to minimise or overcome them.

**See also**
Q10    What are the key barriers to communication?
Q17    When communicating, what should be my primary focus?

## Q12   How can I help people retain my message?

If you pay attention to what is going on inside your head, you will recognise that you are always thinking about something. Your thoughts literally are jumping around like monkeys. As a communicator, you need to remind yourself that that is the reality for your audience as well. Most of us have difficulty concentrating for protracted periods of time, so anything you can do to assist your audience's concentration will serve you better in communicating your message.

One easy way to help people to retain your message is to use verbal images. While a picture may be worth 1,000 words, you can use words to help your audience visualise, if an actual picture is not handy.

For example, a hotelier once described the view from the dining room window of his inn as 'beautiful'. A second hotelier described a view of fields of pink and yellow wild flowers, horses grazing and a rugged mountain rising sharply in the background. Both scenes may be 'beautiful'; but the second description is more memorable.

Whenever possible, use words to create pictures in your audience's minds to aid retention.

**See also**
**Q10**   What are the key barriers to communication?
**Q11**   How can I minimise the barriers to communication?
**Q20**   How important are my choice of words, facts or analogies?
**Q91**   How can I help my audience retain information?

## Q13 Why is listening important?

Most of us take the act of listening for granted. We don't pay attention to our ability to hear until we cannot. "What was that?", "What did he say?", "I didn't hear what you said" or "I've never heard that before!".

Listening is, in fact, a skill to be cultivated. Most of us need to learn to listen, to pay genuine attention to what we hear because we can learn, consider and possibly make changes as a consequence. For some, taking notes helps us to concentrate.

What people say to you or to each other provides you with information about themselves, about their organisation, about their products and services and about their likes and dislikes. Listening keeps you and your organisation informed. It provides you with valuable data you can get in few other ways and helps you to decide whether to make changes.

Unfortunately, too often, we are inattentive, or we are focused on our own work or responsibilities, or we think we are being criticised when we are given information about our ideas, behaviours or our performance. People tend to consider negative information as 'criticism' and thus as harmful and hurtful. But if you think of it as 'feedback', it seems more benign. Feedback provides opportunities for us to develop and enhance our work and our abilities. Welcome it and listen for it.

Encourage your colleagues and employees to listen, to pay attention to what others are saying or writing about the way you do business. Then weigh what you have heard and see whether there is validity in it and how you might change something that you, your department or your company are doing.

**See also**
Q14   Why should I ask for feedback?
Q15   How should I use feedback?
Q100  To continue to improve as a communicator, what kind of feedback should I look for?

## Q14    Why should I ask for feedback?

You can sit in a meeting or walk down the corridor and overhear what people are saying, but being assertive about acquiring feedback helps you too.

Get in the habit of asking for feedback. Ask others for their opinions. What did they think of your talk? What did they think about the recommendations that you made? Did they read your memo? What was their reaction to what you wrote? Ask them why they rejected your idea. What didn't they understand? Who was the best speaker at a conference? Why? How did the meeting go?

In other words, actively seek feedback about your work, about your organisation, about clients' attitudes or consumers' reactions. And probe. Ask for clarification. And encourage others to do the same.

Keep in mind that we always should be striving to improve and to move toward excellence. We are all learning. So, ask yourself how you are doing and do the same for anyone you supervise. Some organisations appraise their employees on a regular basis; others don't. Whether your company uses a formal or informal appraisal system, evaluating whether you are an 'effective communicator' is important. Perhaps such a category or characterisation should be included in the appraisal, addressing issues like speaking, writing and listening.

**See also**
Q15    How should I use feedback?
Q100  To continue to improve as a communicator, what kind of feedback
         should I look for?

# Q15    How should I use feedback?

Simply reflect on it. If you are listening to others and diligently asking questions, you can collect data about your own communication style by sifting through their feedback. And you can do the same for others.

Remember *The Emperor's New Clothes*? In that story, people were afraid to tell the truth because the Emperor was … the emperor. People may be reluctant to share what they perceive to be negative lest they hurt your feelings, damage their relationship or risk their jobs. You want to encourage feedback and you want it to be as specific as possible. Phrases like: "You were great!", "Well done!" or "Nice job" don't move you or anyone else toward a specific goal. You need to probe and ask, "Why do you say that?", "What did I do right?, "Why is that a problem?" or "Do you have a recommendation?". If you hear the same specific feedback often, consider that it may be valid.

Unfortunately, many people choose not to seek feedback because they see any negative news as some sort of failing or as a personal attack. However, when given well and interpreted wisely, feedback can be useful.

And don't assume that only management has valuable insights. Different people in different jobs have different perspectives. Solicit their opinions and think about what they say. Even a minor change may enable you or your organisation to be more effective. Reflect on what you learn and incorporate appropriate changes into your business communication. Then seek feedback on the changes – and so on.

**See also**
Q4     How might my communication style affect business relationships?
Q14    Why should I ask for feedback?
Q100   To continue to improve as a communicator, what kind of feedback should I look for?

## Q16    Why is preparation key to communication?

If your goal is for your audience to think about your message and to respond to it, then you need to minimise the chances for failed communication.

Unclear messages can block communication. To prevent that, you must take time to be clear. You must prepare. Many people pride themselves on being more effective because they are spontaneous and 'off the cuff'. They believe themselves to be more 'real'. Of course, you cannot control a phone conversation – perhaps that's why people prefer them to email – but you certainly can find a few minutes beforehand to reflect on what you want to share and the implications of your ideas.

Suppose you want to discuss the issue of lateness with some members of your staff. Before you begin to draft memos or call meetings about lateness, take the time to determine precisely what aspect(s) of lateness you want to address:

- Do you want to discuss the impact of tardiness on other workers in specific departments?

- Do you want to recommend a new policy because lateness is affecting the morale of people who are coming in on time?

- Do you want to implement a policy to progressively discipline those individuals who are coming in late?

Preparation enables you to refine your thoughts and be clearer, which should result in more effective communication.

**See also**
Q2    Why is clarity essential for effective communication?
Q10   What are the key barriers to communication?
Q11   How can I minimise the barriers to communication?
Q17   When communicating, what should be my primary focus?

## Q17    When communicating, what should be my primary focus?

The audience. The audience. The audience.

You are not the focus of your communication. It's all about the recipients. It's all about the audience. Too often, as humans with foibles, anxieties and idiosyncrasies, we get caught up in our own concerns. How will I sound? How will I look? As communicators, we can be self-absorbed, being more concerned with how anxious or nervous we may appear rather than expending our energy thinking about the audience and what we want to communicate to them.

Focus on the audience and articulate your message as accurately as possible with that unique group or individual in mind.

You would not knowingly speak Japanese to an audience that understands no Japanese, display paintings to the sightless, or play music to the deaf. In the same way, you should not forget that some jargon, certain technical vocabulary, specific images, gestures and words may not be understood or interpreted in the same way by everyone. (As an American in Ireland, it took some time for me to understand shop assistants who asked, "Are you OK?".)

Always start with – and keep – your audience in mind.

### See also
**Q16**    Why is preparation key to communication?
**Q19**    What should I learn about my audience?
**Q66**    Why do I need to think about specific readers when writing?

# BUSINESS COMMUNICATION TECHNIQUES

## Q 18    How important is it for me to be able to articulate my purpose?

It is essential. To be sure your communication is not blocked, you should think through and be able to articulate in one sentence precisely what you are trying to accomplish with your note, fax, memo, report, email or phone call. Ask yourself, 'what do I want as a result?' *Exactly what.*

Remember you are trying to communicate a message to produce a desired outcome. Perhaps you are:

- Motivating staff to complete a task as quickly as possible;
- Discouraging divisiveness;
- Encouraging teamwork;
- Justifying your recommendation or an expenditure;
- Explaining a procedure or policy that has caused confusion;
- Provoking competition between teams or divisions;
- Empathising with someone's predicament;
- Clarifying a situation; or
- Rectifying an error.

You should know exactly why you are writing memos and emails or giving a presentation. You should know the purpose of your reports, your talks and your conversations – not in vague generalities but in as specific terms as you can.

You need to ask yourself why you are addressing the issue. If you don't know, if you can't articulate your purpose, then don't be surprised when people leave your meeting asking each other, "What was *that* all about?". Rather than having resolved a problem, recommended a solution or motivated a different behaviour, your audience may be pondering – or worse yet – dismissing your intentions.

Be clear in your own mind what you expect to accomplish. Know your purpose.

**See also**

**Q2** Why is clarity essential for effective communication?

**Q10** What are the key barriers to communication?

**Q17** When communicating, what should be my primary focus?

## Q19    What should I learn about my audience?

The answer is as much as you can. Know your audience and, if it is written work, think about who might become your audience as well. Who else other than the addressee might receive copies of your reports or emails?

Do your own mini-demographic study. This isn't major research; it takes only a few minutes to acquire the information. Whether you are dealing with an individual, small groups or large one, learn who they are:

- What are their names? Job titles? Nationalities? Native languages?
- Is your audience male? Female? Mixed?
- What are their ages?
- What is their education or experience level?
- What do they know about you, your organisation, its structure and your subject?

In addition to some hard facts, try, if you can, to find out about some of the intangibles. What can you learn about personalities, about ambitions, motivations or frustrations? Be aware of your audience's relationship to you, to the organisation, to the field and to each other. Are there any individual or group dynamics, or any internal or external politics, you should be aware of?

Obtaining this information helps you to tailor your thoughts specifically to the audience and enables you to make explanations that might be more meaningful to them than if you had no knowledge whatsoever. And you can be more sensitive to unspoken patterns of influence and the role that personality may play.

Once you have that information, you should use it. For example, suppose you are an instructor who wants to explain the negotiation process to a group of undergraduates, would you use the example of purchasing a house? While it may be a splendid example, given your knowledge of the audience, negotiating to borrow the family car or to take a semester off college might be a more appropriate choice. The more relevant you can be to your unique audience, the more likely it is that they will grasp and hopefully act on your concepts.

The bottom line: the more you know about your audience, the more you increase the odds of being effective in your communication.

**See also**
Q17    When communicating, what should be my primary focus?
Q30    How can I prepare for an emotional audience?
Q66    Why do I need to think about specific readers when writing?

## Q20    How important are my choice of words, facts or analogies?

They matter. Learn what you can about the person on the other end of the phone, across the desk from you or in front of the computer on the other side of the world. When you communicate with any of them, try to make the best choices you can about how you are going to say what you want to say. And listen carefully.

You may decide to use words in your message rather than images or a combination of both. You may choose a particular language: English, French, German or Chinese. Having done so, then select the precise words that you believe will be best understood by the other parties. For example, if you are talking about computer technologies to people who are not computer-literate, it is unwise to assume that they know all the terminology. Prepare to take the time to explain terms. However, if you are talking to people who have been intimately involved with technological advances over the last 20 years, in-depth explanations may be unnecessary.

In the same way, if you discuss procedural issues that date back five years and your audience consists of people who are new to the organisation, then to help their understanding, it might be useful to provide some background. If, on the other hand, they are senior people, a brief recap, rather than an in-depth background, might be more than adequate. In addition, if you use terms that are idiomatic to your culture, non-natives may not understand. While in Ireland you may say that you are putting an issue 'on the long finger', in the US you must put it on 'the back burner'.

The more you think about the nature, education and experience of your audience, the better your choices will be. The more appropriate your choices, the greater the likelihood that your message will be understood.

### See also
Q10    What are the key barriers to communication?
Q19    What should I learn about my audience?

# Q21    Is there an ideal way to deliver a message?

While there is no perfect method that works on every occasion, the formula involves knowing what you want to say, why you want to say it and who you are saying it to and then deciding on the best way to communicate that information.

To do that, always focus on your audience. Think about the numbers, personalities, issues, politics, knowledge, relationships, diversity, immediacy, confidentiality and distance. Then, given all those variables, consider how best to transmit your message. This analytical process may take you only a few minutes, but it is time well spent. Choosing the wrong medium may delay or impact the outcome.

Decide whether your message is essential for everyone you work with or just for some. Should your ideas be sent by email or distributed by memo to heads of departments? Or would a meeting of the heads of departments be better? Are there any risks involved in sending your message electronically? Does what you are sharing require an opportunity for clarification or is it a simple announcement? Are the notions complex? Will the implications of your message have a different impact on different people?

Decide whether you want to create an opportunity for open discussion. Consider whether it is important that people hear your voice or see your face. Is this a webinar? Do you need to record your remarks in order to best present your ideas? Can someone else say it or do it for you? Would it be better to make a phone call?

Based on the nature of your message and on the composition of your audience, make an informed decision about how you will send your message.

### See also
Q8     After the message and the coding, what else can I control?
Q22    Is there an ideal way to deliver bad news?
Q23    How best can I deliver unsettling messages?

# Q22    Is there an ideal way to deliver bad news?

Communicating is ultimately about the message – and, at times, our messages are not happy ones. If you are conveying negative information, such as about plant closures, lay-offs, or denials of requests, put yourself in the other person's shoes.

Empathise. Imagine how you would receive the message if it were written or said to you.

The usual pattern in relaying bad news is to say something positive first, then to relate the negative information. This approach takes some of the sting out of the bad news. The closing sentence might speak to your continued long-term relationship – whatever that might be.

Bad news is bad news and shouldn't be glossed over, but it should be handled with sensitivity and awareness of its impact on the recipient.

**See also**
Q21    Is there an ideal way to deliver a message?
Q23    How best can I deliver unsettling messages?
Q32    Why does being empathetic matter?

## Q23    How best can I deliver unsettling messages?

Change is difficult for us, even small changes. Try wearing your watch or a bracelet on the opposite wrist for a while and notice your level of discomfort and the time it takes to adjust to this minor change.

As a communicator, one strategy to consider is to give the good news first to soften the blow, then to follow up with the bad news.

Another is to frame your message in terms of opportunities rather than as threats.

And, if you think that your message may cause distress or anxiety, be prepared to handle some of the concerns that the audience as a whole or as individuals may have. For example, if you think that people may feel that your message may lessen their workload and that they may be concerned about the risk of being laid off, speak about those issues. Or if your staff may be concerned about having to work with new people or in ways that are unfamiliar to them, and as a consequence they may feel insecure, again articulate that you appreciate their discomfort.

In addition, people with different jobs often have different perspectives on issues: a union representative may interpret your ideas differently than an accountant; the reactions of newer board members may differ from those of more senior members. Anticipate how differing constituencies or individuals may interpret what you are communicating.

Present your arguments with your audience's concerns in mind. Be politically aware. Give them good news as well as bad and try to help them see as an opportunity what they may perceive to be a threat.

**See also**
Q21    Is there an ideal way to deliver a message?
Q22    Is there an ideal way to deliver bad news?

## Q24    How much information should I include?

When you organise your thoughts, determine what is essential to your message and what is not. Eliminate the extraneous. Too often reports, conversations, memos and talks are filled with information designed to impress rather than to advance the arguments. The extra material may make the report appear weighty or the speaker sound important; however, wordiness can confuse what you want to present clearly.

When you know what you are communicating and why, then decide what you need to include to make your point. Nothing else. Certainly a good story or anecdote may lighten the moment, but if it isn't relevant, let it go. It distracts.

In writing, if you have pages filled with charts and graphs, ask yourself what purpose each one serves. If they don't support or clarify your point, then don't use them. File them for future use. Put them in an appendix, so that readers can look at them without interrupting the flow of their reading. Stick to your point.

What is true for reports is equally true for other forms of communication. When you write an email, how much time do you spend on items other than the one that you want to address? Make your point(s) and eliminate extraneous information.

**See also**
**Q25**    How much background information should I provide?

## Q25 How much background information should I provide?

How much background information to provide is another decision for you to make. When you are organising your thoughts, it is important to bring your audience into the picture by establishing the context for your ideas, recommendations or requests. Therefore, early in your communication, provide the individual or individuals with enough information to allow them to understand what is about to follow.

Always remember that we are all thinking all the time – not necessarily about work-related issues. Your audience may be thinking about other issues: calls to return, emails to write, budgets to finish or videos to return, weight to lose, the colour of your dress, tie or hair, and whether they should consider having lasik surgery or wondering if you have, because you don't wear glasses – and on and on. So, you need to help them focus, and by providing context you do so. When you say, "I need this report sent to ... because...", the 'because' helps the other person to understand the importance or urgency of your request.

Think about the opening scenes of films and TV shows. Filmmakers bring you into the story quickly using a number of methods: for example, you first may see a city from the air. Then the camera focuses on landmarks: the Eiffel Tower, the Houses of Parliament, or the Washington Monument. They have established where you are. Then the camera moves into the streets, perhaps into a particular building, particular sidewalk cafe or into a car. Once there, you meet the characters and into the story. Other films provide a title for an opening shot indicating the location and the time. Both techniques are designed to bring the audience rapidly into the picture.

Do the same thing. Whatever medium you choose – memo, fax, email, report or talk – always establish the context. It might require as little as a few sentences in your introduction or one PowerPoint slide or as much as an entire chapter in a report.

When you do this, you prepare your audience to focus on your message. Establishing the context provides the audience with enough information to understand how your message connects to what they already know, and thus to be willing and able to grasp it more readily.

**See also**

**Q19**     What should I learn about my audience?

**Q24**     How much information should I include?

## Q26 Why should I avoid speaking *ad lib*?

Although it may seem easier at the time, it is not always sensible to *ad lib*. When you do, it is easy to make promises you cannot keep or say something that you didn't mean or that has an unforeseen impact.

So, if it happens that you cannot deliver on your promises, perhaps because of time or budgetary constraints outside your control, you run the risk of letting people down. You may have raised hopes and then dashed them.

Suppose you are counselling an employee about absenteeism and must decide whether to let the person 'off the hook' or to discipline them. Take a moment to think about the implications of that decision, since you risk setting precedents that you may regret later. How often do you see the media jumping on a politician for some sort of similar gaffe?

The same is true for all your messages. Think about their implications. For instance, are there any economic implications to your ideas? Might you offend someone with your remarks? Are you revealing bias towards a particular group? Will you be perceived as pulling a flanker on your boss? Are you telling a half-truth? Did you fail to consider a new regulation?

Because managers are role models, consider whether you would be proud of others emulating you. Would you be embarrassed or angry if your subordinates imitated you? To avoid miscommunication, anger, frustration or embarrassment, think about the implications of your messages. Of course, we are human and we err, but take a deep breath and reflect about the impact, outcome and/or implications of your message before you start to communicate.

**See also**
**Q16** Why is preparation key to communication?
**Q84** How important is practising my presentation?

## Q27    How should I order my thoughts?

To enable your listeners or readers to walk away with a clear understanding of what you are sharing and to help them retain your information, it is helpful to create a structure for your idea or ideas, just as architects create plans for buildings.

Analyse your message to see whether it can be divided into segments. It is easier to take bites of a sandwich than to gulp it down whole. In the same way, it is easier to comprehend the whole by understanding the parts.

The most basic structure that we understand usually includes a beginning, middle and an end (or an introduction, the body and a conclusion). The beginning sets the context or introduces the material; the middle develops the ideas; and the end restates your position or underlines its importance. It's the old advice to speakers: say what you are going to say, say it and then say you have said it.

Suppose you are preparing a series of recommendations. As you work on them, you notice that some relate to budget, others to staffing and still others to policy. Consider creating three categories with those headings – budgetary, staffing and policy – and then fit your recommendations into each of them. In your introduction, explain that you will be making three kinds of recommendations – budgetary, staffing and policy. Thus, your audience is prepared to learn about the three kinds of recommendations. You have helped them follow your logic. And if you are doing this orally, and your audience is seated across the room from you, they may jot down the three headings on a piece of paper or on their laptops. As a result, they may more readily understand or follow your arguments for each of your recommendations.

At the end, remember to recap. Restate your original point. Even in a chat, which may easily move to other subjects, be sure that the other person leaves your office with your message clearly in mind. Be sure to repeat or underline your message before you shake hands and say, "Thanks for coming by".

When creating a structure for your message, you might want to consider some of these tried and tested options:

- **Order of importance:** Suppose you have three key points, arguments or justifications. Decide which of the three is the most important and which is the least. Present your most important idea first, your weakest point second and your second most important last or *vice versa*. Remember we tend to remember beginnings and endings better than the middles, so put your most important argument first or last and your weakest in the middle. What you are doing is what news programmes do. Typically, they begin and end with headlines. Why? They want to grab our attention immediately at the start of the programme and to remind us of what they told us in the recap at the end;

- **Numbering:** You might indicate in your email that you have three questions or points or you tell someone that you have x number of complaints. One of the most effective speeches I have ever heard was someone who announced that he was going to explain 18 changes that were about to affect the tourism industry in that country. As I looked around the audience, everyone was writing '1 to 18' and was prepared to make notes on each item. I copied his approach and, to this day, people say to me "I still remember you giving 18 points on …". After all this time, I am not sure that they recall the actual 18 points, but certainly the strategy for helping recall worked. And be sure to say or write '1', then '2', then '3' to reinforce your numbering structure;

- **Chronology:** If what you are talking about has to do with planning or with changes or issues that are related to time, you can organise your thoughts by beginning with what occurred in the past. Then continue by referring to the present and conclude with the future – for example, "In the past, we … Now we are …, and in the next five years, we will …". Reverse chronology is another option. That approach involves discussing the present first and then going backwards in time. Again, rather than going randomly going forward and backwards, you have ordered your information to help the listener or reader understand it better;

- **Spatially:** Suppose you are an architect or you are discussing distribution of your product or an office redesign. Organise your material so that your analysis moves from the left to the right, right to left, top to bottom, bottom to top, back to front, east to west, north to the south or big to small. The argument is the same, but it is easier for your audience to follow your thinking;

- **Mnemonics:** Another way to organise your ideas is by creating or using memory devices. For those of you who play an instrument, you were probably asked to remember, 'Every Good Boy Does Fine' for the lines on the treble clef. You can do the same thing. Simply look at the key words in your message. Then take the first letter from each of those words and identify a single word made up of those letters that encapsulates what you are saying. For example, your four points might be health, opportunity, purpose and economics. So, you ask the audience to remember the word or mnemonic, HOPE, the initial letters of each of those words. Be wary though of having such a lengthy or contrived mnemonic that they remember the mnemonic but not what the initials represent;

- **Opposites:** You can organise your thoughts by discussing all the negatives or disadvantages of taking an action in one part of your presentation and then grouping all the positives or advantages in another. You can use 'costs' and 'benefits', 'pros' and 'cons', whatever works in your situation.

Which organising technique you use doesn't matter, but having one does. So, take the time to organise your thoughts – sequencing helps the audience follow your thinking. It's particularly important when your message is complex or lengthy, but can be equally handy even when you are writing an email with more than one point.

**See also**

**Q26**    Why should I avoid speaking *ad lib*?

**Q50**    Why do I need a written agenda for a meeting?

**Q71**    How should I structure a formal report?

## Q28 What should I consider when I use images?

You have heard the expression, 'A picture is worth a thousand words'. It's true. We tend to remember better when we visualise. Try to recall a talk you heard, a meeting you attended or some material you read. What comes to mind? Most of us can recall some image from the experience. You may remember the speaker touching his face, or a slide that he used to make a point, or some vivid language.

Take that recollection to heart. What you recall is most likely what other people do too. We remember pictures. But they need not be actual photographs; they can be verbal expressions. Therefore, when you prepare your communication, try to incorporate examples, images and analogies that are memorable – for example:

- Can you compare a complex situation to something simpler?
- Can you describe a situation so the audience can see it?
- Can you put your numbers and statistics together in such a way that what emerges is more than columns of numbers and figures?
- Can you create a pie chart? Or a bar graph? Can you show comparisons?
- Can you actually use an image rather than a line on the chart?

The more vivid your images, the more the audience will remember. Does your third quarter fiscal report remind you of the sinking of the Titanic? Has the fourth quarter turned around so dramatically that it is a 787 climbing to cruising altitude?

Your objective is to have readers and listeners remember what you want them to recall, be it a recommendation, a reprimand, an appraisal or an update.

One *caveat*: be sure that the images you choose are not more memorable than your message. Burst balloons or ride in on a donkey, if you wish, but will anyone remember what you said? Choose your images, but select them wisely.

**See also**

**Q20**   How important are my choice of words, facts or analogies?
**Q76**   What should I consider when developing visuals?
**Q77**   Why are titles essential for charts and graphs?
**Q78**   How can I make a slide more effective?
**Q79**   How should I use charts and visuals in a report?
**Q89**   Must I include visuals in a talk?
**Q92**   Should I practise with my visuals?

## Q29    How should I factor location and timing into my communication?

Conveying a message to colleagues in a pub is different from conveying the same message in a boardroom. Chatting with a colleague by the water cooler is different from making a presentation to 400 people at a conference in a hotel in Paris. Your audience is comprised of people, and they are human. They have feelings, sensitivities, moods, and differing levels of energy. What is effective on a Friday afternoon may not work on a Monday morning. Just as conveying news about major organisational changes requires a different approach from giving a weekly status report, or what goes into a formal report may be inappropriate for a memo, so too communication over cocktails after a long day's work may be quite different than talk over coffee in the conference room first thing Monday morning. Most trainers will tell you that the worst days to give training sessions are Mondays and Fridays. Why? On Mondays people tend to be a tad down or are coming back to desks laden with responsibilities, and on Fridays folks are beginning to wind down and focus on their plans for the weekend.

Consider your message and the setting before deciding on the most appropriate tone, voice, demeanour or clothing choice. Can you determine the setting, or is it prescribed? Are you in a position to say, "Let's meet to talk at such and such a restaurant", or has the conference room already been decided on?

Typically, in terms of the tone you take and the image you present, the more people you address in writing or orally, the more formal you tend to be. However, formality does not mean suddenly becoming stiff, stuffy or using high-flown vocabulary. While you may prefer to appear less casual, when the audience is larger or more remote, you typically have less information about their knowledge base or the personalities of all involved, so you can make fewer assumptions. And they may know less about you, so you may be creating a memorable first impression.

And last, in terms of location, remember that while business now works in a global economy, that global economy comprises lots of local economies, each with their different cultures. A humorous cliché in one culture may be an unforgivable offense in another.

**See also**
**Q10**   What are the key barriers to communication?
**Q82**   What should I look for when I visit the venue in advance of my talk?

## Q30 How can I prepare for an emotional audience?

Understanding your audience goes well beyond analysing demographic data – how many men or women and how old they are. You are working with human beings. As you well know, people are emotional. We have fears, doubts, anxieties, beliefs, and values. Therein lies both a great joy and a source of frustration. You cannot underestimate the importance for a communicator of being sensitive to, and aware of, feelings and beliefs.

No matter how stressful the situation you are in, treat people with respect and dignity. At times, you will have to deal with irate or frustrated colleagues or customers. Under stress, people may shout, rage or weep. Hopefully, you will have anticipated possible emotional reactions to negative news, and you will have built something into your remarks. While you cannot change the content of the message itself, you can be aware of other people's sensitivities. However, if you find yourself to be the subject of an outburst, maintain your own dignity as well as that of the other person. Let them regret losing their cool, while you maintain yours.

It is easy to get caught up in the heat of an argument or to defend your point of view passionately. If you become involved in either situation, try to maintain an objective view of the larger picture. Keep your vision in mind. Remember what you want to achieve. If you don't, you can easily become embroiled in the problems of others. Stay focused on your message. Don't allow yourself to be side-tracked with other people's emotional arguments that move you off your essential points. Stay on the issues at hand. Don't become emotional yourself. It is easy to become angered when others don't appear to be listening to you or are not taking your work seriously. Keep reminding yourself what you want to accomplish. Salespeople face rejection daily, but to be successful they have to keep focused on the next sale. Good communicators do, too. Certainly afterwards reflect on what is being said to you, but during the debate keep your own purpose in mind.

When you are speaking, people may ask you questions that you believe to be stupid, posturing or belligerent. If this happens:

- Allow your questioners to express their feelings in their own way;
- Listen, maintain your own decorum and take the questions seriously. Recognise that, in fact, those people may not want answers. They just may want to get their own messages off their chests;
- Keep focused on your own message;
- Repeat your main points, if necessary, but do not be drawn into verbal fisticuffs;
- Offer to research a contentious point;
- Encourage the combatant to provide you with data at another time.

If they persist or become angry, they, not you, will lose the respect of any other listeners. You gain stature, because you remain calm under fire.

**See also**
**Q19**   What should I learn about my audience?
**Q31**   Why is it important to anticipate objections?
**Q32**   Why does being empathetic matter?
**Q44**   How can I prepare for difficult reactions?

## Q31   Why is it important to anticipate objections?

If you want to win an argument or make a sale, when you organise your thoughts, anticipate the arguments you are likely to hear. Expect people to say that they don't have the time, the money, the interest, the background or the personnel to implement your proposals. Your audience's organisational roles, hobby horses or particular biases *vis-a-vis* you or the company should help you identify some areas of contention and enable you to prepare for their arguments. For example, someone may see your remarks or message as:

- Threatening to their own authority or to one of their pet projects rather than as an opportunity for development;
- Too time-consuming or as non-essential to the effective running of the organisation;
- Personal rather than professional;
- A need for you to show your authority.

The better you know your audience, the more can anticipate some of their objections and prepare your arguments or your answers in advance. "I know that you are very busy right now, but ..." or "I recognise that we are short-handed; however ...", or "I appreciate that we have had to lay off some people and that makes you anxious or saddens you, but ...". In each case with a simple parenthetical, you have anticipated a concern or a current reality. It may soften the blow and encourage acceptance of your requests.

**See also**
**Q32**   Why does being empathetic matter?
**Q44**   How can I prepare for difficult reactions?

## Q32    Why does being empathetic matter?

Good communicators are careful about making inappropriate remarks. Your objective is for your message to reach the other person or persons in your audience. You do not want to lose anyone by being offensive or politically incorrect.

It is easy to offend people with off-colour jokes or by stereotyping. Suppose you refer to a particular nationality as fat or loud, to seniors as decrepit or unable to think for themselves, or all women as cooks and knitters, all consumers as gullible or teenagers as irresponsible, you risk offending someone. Not everyone in that particular country is fat or loud, not all seniors are decrepit, not all consumers are gullible, not all women are cooks and knitters. Someone who hears your remarks may think about them and then about you. They may start asking themselves, "Did you really mean that? Is that the way you feel? Well, my best friend is from that country and she isn't …". Or they identify with the group and silently think to themselves, "I am not irresponsible or loud (or whatever adjective you have used)". What happens in that moment is that the brain of your reader or listener is mulling over the implication of that offhand word. They have stopped paying attention to your message. And you have lost your audience.

A simple slip of a pronoun can make a difference. Some managers always use the pronoun 'I' – but 'I' is exclusive rather than inclusive. Making a simple change from 'I' to 'we' creates a sense of team rather than a sense of separateness. So be aware of your pronouns.

And watch your use of the pronouns 'he' and 'she'. If you are talking about a particular product or service, don't assume that only one sex buys groceries or does the laundry. Not all receptionists are women and not all airline pilots are men. Both men and women are corporate executives.

As you well know, people have strong feelings about the European Union, football, sexuality, divorce, politics and cloning, to name just a few topics. You cannot be aware of every issue that might be emotive to someone. So be cautious about the possibilities of hurting people and thus losing your audience's attention or respect. Avoid casting aspersions, even on the competition. In other words, be aware and be sensitive to others' feelings and values.

**See also**
**Q19**    What should I learn about my audience?
**Q30**    How can I prepare for an emotional audience?
**Q31**    Why is it important to anticipate objections?

## Q33    What's the risk in over-generalising?

By over-generalising, you risk your credibility – and even may offend.

We bristle at an over-generalisation – for example, if a report suggests that all motorway deaths are caused by the drinks industry. When film and television are blamed for all teenage violence, you recognise another generalisation.

Be sure that remarks you make about people or companies can be substantiated with hard data. Be able to prove your case when you identify the cause of an organisational problem. Be sure too that your solution is not over the top either.

The same is true when you are talking to clients: "We have eliminated the design flaw. The problem is gone. The system will work perfectly." Do you know for sure? Have you eliminated all the problems? *All the problems*? Will the system now work properly?

Say only what you can support. Because, if you are challenged, and you cannot provide supporting data to make your case, you risk not only losing your argument but also your credibility.

Instead, be specific when writing or speaking. Rather than indicating that "there has been an upward trend in pricing", be specific – say "prices have risen by 10% in the past six months".

When you are specific, your audience better grasps what you mean and can better evaluate the impact of your remarks on their work. In addition, they can remember your point.

**See also**
**Q35**    Why is it important to fact-check?
**Q75**    What is the difference between a recommendation and a conclusion?

## Q34    Why are analogies useful?

When a report, a talk or an email are too abstract or unclear for us, we may become bewildered, confused, frustrated or disinterested. We stop paying attention, and we start thinking about other things. One of the best ways to keep your audience's attention is to use examples or analogies that help to clarify a complex point. Electronic mail uses words like 'mailbox' or 'address book' to enable us to relate to what initially may have been technologically challenging. Those familiar terms simplified the concept and made our learning curve shorter. Consider using homespun analogies that derive from universal experiences that we have from home, office, shop, sports, or school.

There is one *caveat*, however, which relates to your knowledge of the audience. If you believe that everyone present understands American football, it would be appropriate to illustrate a point by using an analogy from that sport. However, if they are unfamiliar with the game, and rugby is their game of choice, then your decision to describe business strategy in terms of American football may be lost on your audience. Saying that "We are going to make a Hail Mary pass" will mean nothing.

So, analogies are valuable and useful, but as always, the more you think about or know your audience, the better your choice of analogy will be and the more likely it will be that your message will be understood.

**See also**
**Q19**    What should I learn about my audience?

# Q35    Why is it important to fact-check?

Your audience – whether listeners or readers – has a right to expect professionalism from you. Be careful, therefore, of using an inaccurate statistic, of making an error on a graph, of presenting an invalid finding, or of using a wrong name. Inadvertent errors of fact, simple typos or misspelling undermine your efforts to communicate successfully. A single error might lead people to believe you may be guilty of more. So, be careful. Double-check. Triple-check.

Be sure that the words or the images that you are using accurately convey your ideas. If you develop a brochure or website that indicates that every room in your hotel has a window overlooking the sea, then make sure this is true. If only a third of them do, then you cannot say that all the rooms overlook the sea. If you know that the cost will be €200, then say €200 not €175 (with the extra charges hidden in small print).

The same applies to your actions. If you promise to phone a client the next day at 10:00 am and have no intention of doing so, don't promise it. If you believe that your solution for a technical problem will make a difference to everyone in the organisation, say so – but, if you aren't sure, don't. Better yet, identify those areas in which you know your solution may help. You will be believed.

Think about how you felt when you were misled. Being accurate and truthful is about your credibility.

**See also**
**Q33**    What's the risk in over-generalising?

# Q36 How serious is violating confidentiality?

You know the answer to this question: very serious.

Be careful of revealing proprietary information to competitors or to colleagues who are not intended to know about it. If you have completed research that should not be shared, be wary of talking about it.

Of course, sometimes maintaining confidentiality can be difficult to do, especially when you have been immersed in a project. You may have been living with the project for so long that you make an inadvertent reference to some aspect of it, which you subsequently regret when you realise that the material may not be appropriate for everyone's ears or eyes. You want to provide enough information to prove your point to the other person; however, if you violate confidentiality, you may lose their trust and respect – as well as that of your superiors. Such a loss can be costly – in serious situations, you may risk your job or your career. Some information is to be safeguarded and not to be shared; it's proprietary.

Sometimes you are in the awful and uncomfortable position of knowing something that should be shared. Or you have been asked to "say nothing", and you know you should. But confidentiality and your reputation demands that you do not. When you counsel an employee about a problem and agree that the discussion will remain between the two of you, then honour that agreement.

Although office gossip is a fact of life, you don't want to be viewed as someone who shares others' confidences. You would rather be seen as someone with whom anything can be shared because it won't go any further. You can acquire significant information by respecting other people's confidentiality or privacy. Equally, you risk your good name if you repeat confidential information or share a secret.

**See also**
**Q3** How does being an effective communicator affect my personal credibility and professionalism?

## Q37 How can I use my hands and my facial expression to enhance communication?

When we think of communication, we tend to think of written and spoken words; remember that we communicate non-verbally too. Good communicators are sensitive to the impact that their non-verbal behaviour can have on others. As you well know, many of our first impressions are formed before other people speak to us. We make instantaneous judgements when we see people, and something as simple as a strong or a 'dead fish' handshake may cause us to form an opinion of someone's personality.

Because our hands are expressive, they are a valuable and readily available pair of visuals. You can:

- Lift your hands;
- Count on your fingers;
- Describe shapes;
- Heft imaginary weight;
- Clench your fists;
- Open and close your hands;
- Expose your palms.

Use your hands rather than trying to hide them – jamming one or both into your pockets, putting them behind your back, or clasping them in front of you. Try not to fiddle with paper, pens or pencils because you are at a loss as to how to use your hands. Such habits tend to make you appear insecure or threatened. Instead, use your hands to describe and underline your message.

Of course, over-doing it and 'talking with your hands' or making repetitive moves or gestures may be seen to be fidgeting or a reflection of your anxiety.

And avoid pointing at someone with your finger, because that gesture appears threatening – and is offensive in some cultures.

Like your hands, your face can convey a message just as your words do. Even when we are saying nothing, when we listening, our faces convey messages. If we are:

- Surprised or concerned, we raise or knit our eyebrows;

- Delighted, disappointed or dismayed, we turn the corners of our mouths up or down;

- Non-plussed, we may drop our jaws;

- Moved, we may frown, grimace or smile, look quizzical, thoughtful, angry or bewildered.

Rather than thinking that you should be expressionless so as not to distract the audience from your message, quite the contrary, use your face. If you are pleased by what you are saying, smile. If you are concerned, frown. In other words, your face should mirror your words, not contradict them. When you say you are 'delighted to meet' someone, you should appear to be delighted. If you are concerned about third quarter profits, then you should look concerned, not happy.

Your ability to communicate with your hands and face makes you a far more interesting and memorable communicator.

**See also**
Q38    Is there any way to improve my voice?
Q39    Are there rules about how I should stand?
Q40    How do idiosyncratic gestures and pet phrases affect my communication?
Q88    Why is making eye contact with the audience important?
Q97    How can I improve my ability as a communicator?

## Q38    Is there any way to improve my voice?

The truth is that most people have good voices. However, with the exception of trained actors and singers, few of us take full advantage of what we can do when we speak. We can:

- Raise and lower our voices;
- Whisper;
- Laugh;
- Speak swiftly or slowly;
- Stop talking altogether.

Varying what you do when you speak makes what you are saying more interesting to the listener. Ever been barely able to keep your eyes open when you were listening to someone who droned on at the same pitch and pace? Perhaps you've looked around and noticed others in the room actually nodding off. By speeding up, slowing down, raising or lowering your voice, you help maintain interest. In addition, by making changes in your delivery, you can emphasise significant words or phrases or de-emphasise something that is less critical.

Learn to stop from time to time. Pausing is a wonderful and underused technique. A moment of silence gives people time to absorb what you have just said. In addition, it can underline an important point. Also people are startled by silence. In fact, it may help your audience refocus. Silence can be powerful. Next time you listen to an effective speaker, notice what happens when the speaker stops for a few moments.

Depending on the situation, you may use your voice differently. In other words, just as it is annoying to hear someone shouting into their mobile phone, if you have a powerful voice and are speaking in a small room, lower your volume. If you are soft-spoken and are giving a talk in a large room, try slowing down and projecting your voice rather than requesting a microphone. Avoid shouting. When we are nervous, most of us speak quickly, sometimes too quickly. If you catch yourself rushing, consciously slow down.

Our voices have different qualities. Some people are naturally soft-spoken, others bellow. Some people have husky voices; others are more nasal. Some people have strong regional accents that may sound musical but may be difficult for a stranger to understand. Get to know your own voice.

Consider recording yourself to hear how you sound to other people. When you do this, also listen for any extraneous noises that you may make. Do you hear 'tsks', 'ums' or 'ers'? Do you smack your lips together between sentences? Do you pull your tongue off the roof of your mouth and make noise? There's nothing wrong with any of these extraneous noises until your listeners notice them to the exclusion of what you are saying.

Recognising the qualities in your own voice and then taking advantage of your vocal variety enhances your communication because you are more interesting to listen to.

**See also**
**Q37** How can I use my hands and my facial expression to enhance communication?
**Q39** Are there rules about how I should stand?
**Q40** How do idiosyncratic gestures and pet phrases affect my communication?

## Q39    Are there rules about how I should stand?

If you have a video camera, film yourself speaking – just a few minutes will do. If you don't have a camera, find a full-length mirror and stand before it and practise giving a talk. Move around a bit and take a close look at yourself. Do you normally stand tall, with shoulders back and squared and hips parallel to the floor? Or are your shoulders and hips all akimbo? Women who bring up their shoulders and tilt their heads may look coquettish, while men with one hip up and one shoulder up may look like a gunslinger from an old Western movie.

Your objective is to look natural, not like a stick figure or a totem pole. You want to stand tall with your head up. The plus to that position is that you can take more air into your lungs, which enables you to project your voice, and being able to breathe more deeply may have a calming effect.

If you have a video or can watch yourself in a mirror, take a look at what you are doing with your feet. Is your weight balanced evenly on both feet, or do you rock backward and forward on your toes? Do you bounce up and down when you speak? Do you take small dance steps? Do you wrap one foot around the other ankle? Catch yourself if you do. Work on breaking the habit. If you don't, people may focus more on what you are doing with your feet than on your message.

Even if they are giving a formal talk behind a dais, sometimes you can see the speakers' shoulders go up and down when they lift their heels up and down.

And speaking of daises, try to avoid them altogether. Many people think that they are safer behind one. But you are more open and interesting if you don't use them at all. For those of you who are terrified by the notion of being so exposed, try it. Practise walking away from the dais, around the conference table and even into an aisle. When you are speaking, move around the room. A figure in motion can be far more interesting than a static one.

But don't pace back and forth like a caged lion. Move naturally. Walk, stop, get close to some people then walk toward others. The proximity enables you to see reactions better. This is not about invading people's personal space or intimidating them, it is simply about being more interesting. Also, if you tend to speak quickly, walking slows your delivery.

**See also**
Q37   How can I use my hands and my facial expression to enhance communication?
Q38   Is there any way to improve my voice?
Q40   How do idiosyncratic gestures and pet phrases affect my communication?

## Q40    How do idiosyncratic gestures and pet phrases affect my communication?

We are all unique individuals and, when presenting, we may make strange little noises or use the same words over and over again or make ballet movements with our feet. These and other little mannerisms distract our audience and therefore detract from our message.

Ask yourself whether you have ever seen speakers with any of the following habits:

- Tossing their heads trying to keep wayward strands of hair behind their ears or pushing a wayward strand behind an ear?
- Constantly smoothing their hair, their cheek or their ties?
- Keeping nervous fingers busy by playing with a button, the edge of a jacket hem or with keys and coins in their pockets?
- Rocking back and forth or up and down on their heels or twisting their ankles so they are standing on the side of a foot?
- Frequently pushing their glasses up their noses only to have them slip again, thus requiring another push?
- Constantly clearing their throats, rubbing their ears or twirling their hair?

By themselves, each of these behaviours and activities is innocuous. Repeated too often, they will be noticed, and people may begin to focus on them or even count them.

Over time, most of us develop pet phrases, which we repeat. Used occasionally, they are harmless. In fact, if your audience knows you well, they even may anticipate them. However, overly repeated, they can be distracting. The person with whom you are talking or to whom you are speaking begins to focus on their repetition rather than the important message that you have to communicate.

Beware! Pay attention to yourself when you're speaking. Notice these repeated behaviours and phrases. Catch yourself using them. Then try to stop or at least ration their use.

It might be a good idea to ask a friend or a colleague whether you have any such habits. If you do, you can work on eliminating them. Remember that mannerisms you have developed over years take time to disappear. Be patient and persistent.

**See also**

**Q37**  How can I use my hands and my facial expression to enhance communication?

**Q38**  Is there any way to improve my voice?

**Q39**  Are there rules about how I should stand?

## Q41    What does my workspace say about me?

Take a hard look at your workspace. True, we all work in different environments and have different types of jobs. Some of us prefer to have desks or tables with nothing on them. Others have desks covered with books, CDs, flash drives, files and papers. Whichever way you prefer to work, you should be able to find what you are seeking with ease.

*Look at your desk.* Do you see any confidential files open for anyone to read? Are phone messages and unopened mail strewn across your desk? Do you have notes lying around that should have been filed or thrown away? Are there crumpled papers? Are there handouts from presentations from two years ago? Are there dated samples?

*Look at the walls.* Do you have photographs or framed sayings that might offend others? If you have a calendar, is the current month showing? Do you have an 'ego wall' covered with your awards and degrees, diplomas and certificates? Do you need them all? Who are they for? For you? Or for the person who comes into your office? What kind of pictures do you have? Why? What effect might they have on others?

*Look around.* Do you have old coffee cups, drinks cans, or empty water bottles strewn about? Are greasy paper bags or yoghurt containers from old lunches in sight? Are papers coffee-stained?

If this is a picture of your office, consider the impression that it might make on another person. Even in an electronic age, while you may think that all that paper makes you look busy, a visitor may perceive you to be careless, disorganised, understaffed or sloppy.

In addition, note how you have arranged your office. Is it friendly? In other words, if you someone wants to talk to you, can they sit somewhere? Or do they have to stand? If there is room, how are chairs positioned? Across the desk from you? Beside your desk? Do you always talk to people while you are sitting behind your desk, making you appear protected or unapproachable? Can you move to a small table? Or can you go to a conference room?

In other words, look at your desk, your walls, your work and recognise that they project an image of you. And then ask yourself whether it is the image you want to project. A minor adjustment, a change of picture or the removal of post-its stuck on your computer screen may make a difference.

**See also**
**Q42**    What does my paperwork say about me?
**Q43**    What image does my organisation project?

## Q42    What does my paperwork say about me?

Take a look at what leaves your office with your name on it, be it an email, or a typed report. Then ask yourself whether it reflects the image that you want to project.

Think about how your paperwork might appear to others. And if and when you have to give a talk, what do you use for notes? A page torn from a refill pad? Or actual note cards? And when your talk is done, do you leave the page crumpled up on the conference table, or do you take your notes away with you?

When you take a phone message for someone, do you write it on a pad? Or do you write it on the handiest white space available, even if it is the cover of the budget or a formal report? Just think about it.

You project your image with the documents that leave your office or organisation. Think about how documents that are produced by your organisation appear to other people. Do all the outgoing letters look different, or do they have the same format?

You may want to consider developing a 'house style'. Having one means that you have determined the lay-out, font, spacing, headings, bullets, use of white space, cover page, binders and binding. That effort at consistency should create professional-looking documents.

Make sure that your business cards are designed with the same care and thoughtfulness. Are they simple and clear and say what you need them to say?

**See also**
**Q41**    What does my workspace say about me?
**Q43**    What image does my organisation project?

## Q43 What image does my organisation project?

If you are asking this question, then you are a part of an organisation. Whether it is made up of one or two people, or employs thousands, whether it is profit or not-for-profit, that organisation should appear as attractive and professional as its individual members do.

What does your company communicate? To answer this question, go beyond the expensive brochures or creative logos. Take a walk. Pretend you are a visitor. Look at the street outside or your parking area, the entrance or the reception desk. What is the first thing you see? Are windows and doors clean? Are signs clear and attractive? When you enter the building, what do you see? Old newspapers or today's? Ashtrays with sweet wrappers or dishes filled with sweets? Are the plants wilted, or cared for? Is the receptionist or first person you meet courteous with everyone or with just the so-called 'important' people? Are you greeted with a smile and made comfortable or are you ignored? Is the office dirty and dusty-looking, or is it clean? Do the people in the office have long faces or are they pleasant-looking? Are bins full of trash? Do employees smile and acknowledge strangers, or are they too self-absorbed? Are lavatories available and supplied?

Attractive offices and welcoming people send out a positive message, while sloppy offices and people with poor attitudes send negative ones. Remember to look for the unwritten messages that your organisation communicates. Your corporate image can turn off your audience or send a message of professionalism that welcomes them with open arms.

**See also**
**Q41** What does my workspace say about me?
**Q42** What does my paperwork say about me?

## Q44    How can I prepare for difficult reactions?

Whether you are coaching a staff member or talking with a potential client, effective communicators are sensitive to reaction, are aware of differing interpretations of what they wish to say and anticipate the reaction. Once you know what you want to say and how, before you go any further, put yourself in the audience's place. Ask yourself, "Will they accept what I want to communicate?". Just as effective salespeople anticipate objections and prepare to overcome them, you should too.

In other words, prepare for possible arguments you might encounter. Think through what you are saying and consider how your audience – one or many – might react. Are you sharing ideas that take time to absorb? Is your concept complex? Will any part of the message confuse or overwhelm? Might there be an emotional outburst, either of joy or dismay? Will you meet with resistance? Will you be asked to defend or justify your ideas? Will any numbers, percentages or statistical data that you are sharing be 'information overload'?

Think through how you might handle the reaction. Have a couple of ready answers in your pocket. Indicate that you will get back with more details, or that you have the research or data available for them to look at.

The best way to anticipate emotional responses is to be empathetic. Put yourself in your audience's shoes. Recognise that some people may be worried, delighted or angered in advance of hearing your ideas or devastated after hearing them. Is an employee with a large family frightened that they may be laid off or are you asking someone to stay late? Are you leaving? Retiring? Relocating? Are you handing over a pet project to someone else? Or dropping it? Will shareholders attend a meeting already angry because of the past performance of the company? Or will they attend delighted by past performance, expect to hear more good news and thus be unable or unwilling to hear negative information that may affect profits?

Anticipate that your messages may require significant background information.

Before uttering a sound or writing a word, consider how your audience will receive your message. Will you worry the audience? Will you delight them? Will some people become nervous, while others relax? The more you anticipate reaction, the less likely that your ideas will be met with bewilderment or anger.

**See also**
**Q25**    How much background information should I provide?
**Q30**    How can I prepare for an emotional audience?
**Q32**    Why does being empathetic matter?
**Q45**    Why should I welcome complaints?

## Q45    Why should I welcome complaints?

It is easy to be annoyed or angered by customers, clients or colleagues when they complain about something you have done. You may feel resentful or unappreciated. You may feel that they haven't understood your position and lack all the facts relating to the situation. When someone has something negative to share, hard as it is to do, try to turn that visceral reaction around and view the complaint as an opportunity. Perhaps there *is* validity in what is being said.

Consider, too, that the individual has taken the time or had the courage to come forward and express a concern or disappointment about a person, a product, a procedure or a policy. Applaud the fact that you have created a culture that supports and encourages openness.

Unfortunately, most of us complain to each other rather than to the party who can do something about the problem. So, when a colleague or client comes forward to express an opinion, you have the opportunity to learn about a problem that may need remedying or that reveals a level of discontent or disappointment.

Thank the individual for bringing the matter to your attention, reflect on what has been told to you, and if there is validity and the issue is remediable, then indicate what steps you intend to take. Avoid false hope or promises that you cannot keep.

And, if you say that you are going to look into the matter or that you are going to remedy it, keep your word.

**See also**
**Q14**    Why should I ask for feedback?
**Q15**    How should I use feedback?
**Q44**    How can I prepare for difficult reactions?
**Q100**    To continue to improve as a communicator, what kind of feedback should I look for?

## Q46 In a high-speed electronic world, is there time for courtesies?

Even though life and business seem to be happening faster, and more and more activities are performed *via* the Internet or by texting, little things still mean a lot when you are dealing with people. People remember the graciousness of others or their lack of it. People value "Good morning", "Good-bye", "Thank you" and "Please". Those words don't take up so much time that they impede your progress. But being courteous goes beyond simply saying "Please" and "Thank you".

Have you ever:

- Been yawned at or heard someone chewing gum or munching on a sandwich over the telephone?
- Been kept on hold listening to music and no one came back to see if you were still waiting or to thank you for holding?
- Walked into a shop or office and been ignored by the shop assistants or receptionists while they finish or continue their personal chats?
- Have you ever applied for a position or submitted a proposal, sent in or emailed a CV and then never heard another word?
- Have you ever sent a memo seeking feedback and received none?
- Have you ever covered the reception desk and been ignored by colleagues who walk by?
- Have you ever joined a small group of people and have no one take responsibility for making introductions?

These are all unfortunate lapses of courtesy, but they could be avoided, if people realised how important courtesies can be and how inexpensive they are to instil.

Try to slow your life down enough to remember the courtesies or remind your staff what a difference a smile and a "Thank You" can make. When people do something for you, don't take it for granted. Say "Thank you".

A personal touch matters to others and may produce more generosity in return.

So, when you indicate that you will get back to someone with information in a week's time, it is common courtesy to do what you promised. In a week's time, phone or email providing what you promised, indicating that there will be a delay, or regretting your ability to fulfil your commitment. You are respecting other people when you are polite. While new technology may be replaced quickly with even newer technology, these little messages still mean so much, perhaps even more when we live and work at such a hectic pace.


**See also**

**Q3**     How does being an effective communicator affect my personal
           credibility and professionalism?

**Q4**     How might my communication style affect business relationships?

# MEETINGS & INTERVIEWS

## Q47     How can I get the best from an informal meeting?

We probably have more informal meetings than formal ones. Informal meetings happen any time or any place. You may be walking down the street and see a colleague or notice clients having lunch at the same restaurant you are, or you might stop by someone's desk or cubicle, or casually chat over a pint at a pub or a latte at a coffee shop. We see people we work with or for in informal settings all the time. And frequently, after the opening social gambit, a conversation begins with, "Do you have a minute?" or "Do you mind coming by my office?" or "Delighted to have bumped into you because I have been meaning to ask," or "I have been wanting to share something with you".

These can be wonderful opportunities; however, you need to decide whether to avail of the moment. The timing or the location may suggest that you want to keep the moment light or social, and that it is not the time to discuss an individual's termination or to challenge someone's underlying assumption about declining revenue.

But if you sense that the timing is appropriate, and you have a question to ask, an issue to put right, a problem to be resolved or presented, then seize the moment – particularly, if the other person frequently is caught up with other issues.

Try to keep the exchange simple. Be aware that listening may be difficult, depending on where you are. The environment may not be quiet; mobiles may ring; text messages may disrupt. Those interruptions distract, and invariably we end up, "Oh, I lost my train of thought"'.

And delighted as you may be to have the opportunity for a discussion, avoid raising too many issues or rolling out a lengthy agenda. Stay on your message – stick to one or two issues – largely because you are relying on memory, theirs and yours.

If you can, if the circumstances permit, take a few notes. If not, take notes as soon as possible after the meeting ends, summarising what was said, and email them to the person with whom you were speaking to be sure that you both recall correctly what was said. Then you can make your action plan – which may require a formal meeting.

**See also**
**Q48**   How can I get the best from a formal meeting?

## Q48     How can I get the best from a formal meeting?

If it is your meeting, who to include is important for you to consider as well as in what location. Other points for you to consider are the timing and length of the meeting and the order of topics.

If you are a participant at the meeting, you should be prepared not only regarding the material, but also to listen, to ask questions and to take notes in whatever way helps you to retain information.

For most formal meetings, agendas are distributed at least a few days in advance. Having the agenda in advance allows you to become familiar with or to prepare for the issues under discussion. So, if you see an item that is new to you, or one on which you want to make a point, you have an opportunity to do some research or to have someone provide briefing notes for you.

At the meeting itself, as a participant, you should rely not only on your listening skills, but also on whatever method helps you retain information. Some people use laptops or iPads to write notes; others use a pad and pen. If a question occurs to you while someone else is speaking, it's often helpful to write down your question, so that you are not so distracted by trying to remember what you want to say that you miss hearing what other people are saying.

Don't be bashful. If you cannot hear what someone has said or if the meaning of what someone has said is unclear to you, there is no harm in asking the chairperson to have the person repeat what was said or to clarify their comments by way of an example.

Stay focused. Sometimes, at meetings, the person seated beside you may want to comment privately to you about something that has been said. Without being rude, ask them to hold the thought until later, because you are listening. You know how hard it is to stay on track when someone is having a side-conversation with you.

And unless seats are assigned, take the seat that works best for you – where you can see the screen if one is in use, or the speaker so you can watch their body language as well as listen to their words. Rather than playing power games about where to sit, locate yourself where you can hear, where you can take the notes you need and where you can be seen (important if you plan to speak during the meeting). At a large meeting, place yourself within easy reach of any standing microphone or of the person who is holding a handheld roving microphone.

**See also**

Q47    How can I get the best from an informal meeting?
Q49    How should I prepare for a formal meeting?
Q50    Why do I need a written agenda for a meeting?
Q51    How important is the length and timing of a meeting?

## Q49    How should I prepare for a formal meeting?

Formal meetings take time from your schedule and from other people's schedules too – not just the time allocated for the meeting itself, but for preparation and travel also. To be effective, they require preparation.

If you are in charge of the meetings, use Kipling's 'six honest servingmen' to help you prepare:

- **What:** What topics do you want to include (or exclude) and in what order?
- **How:** How much time will you allocate to each topic?
- **Why:** Why hold the meeting? What do you want to achieve by the end?
- **When:** When will you hold the meeting? And when will you announce it?
- **Where:** Where will you hold the meeting?
- **Who:** Last, but definitely not least, who will attend it?

By preparing the agenda, you decide what topics the meeting will consider and your choice of order indicates the importance you attach to each topic. Once the preliminaries are out of the way, it is usual to focus on the key topics before turning to less important issues. Of course, new topics may be added under 'Any Other Business' but your choice essentially determines the structure of the meeting and is reinforced by the time you allocate to each topic during the meeting. What exactly do you want to discuss? What don't you want to discuss? How many issues are there? Who is going to provide the background, if at all, and how much time will it take?

As you prepare the agenda, think about what you want to achieve by the meeting's end. Do you want to reach a decision – by consensus, or majority vote? Do you simply want to hear participants' views on the topic – to be summarised with a view to presenting a recommendation at the next meeting?

Since the timing and the location of a meeting can have an impact on the participants, you need to decide carefully on both. Do you call a meeting for first thing on Monday morning, or for Friday afternoon? Is mid-week better for some participants' travel commitments? Do you hold it after lunch or in the morning? Or is it a meeting that you have every week, month, or day at the same time in the same place? And when choosing a location, consider not just travel access and cost, but also the layout of the room? Is a classroom-style arrangement around a conference table appropriate? Or do you need a more relaxed layout, around a small coffee table? Is the group so large that you will need a microphone for speakers to be heard? Will you need to set up a telephone or video link with someone in a different location who is unable to attend in person? If so, make sure all of this is handled in advance.

If your meeting is a regular event, you only need to remind participants of venue, location and time. But if it's a once-off, perhaps you need to consider when to announce it. How much notice will participants need to fit it into their schedules? Or is attendance compulsory, so participants will be expected to reschedule other commitments?

Last, you need to decide who should attend. Often, the nature of the meeting or the topics to be covered determines who the participants should be. It's important to make sure everyone who needs to participate is invited, without casting your net so widely that you waste people's time on matters that don't really concern them. But remember that a person who needs to attend your meeting to participate in the discussion of a specific topic need not attend for the full meeting – just the part that concerns them.

If you are not in charge, but simply a participant, your preparation for a meeting begins once you receive your invitation and the agenda. Use the time before the meeting to become familiar with, or prepare for, the issues under discussion. If you see an item that is new to you, or one on which you want to make a point, you have an opportunity to do some research or to have someone provide briefing notes for you.

**See also**

**Q48**   How can I get the best from a formal meeting?
**Q50**   Why do I need a written agenda for a meeting?
**Q51**   How important is the length and timing of a meeting?

## Q50 Why do I need a written agenda for a meeting?

First, it is not always necessary to have a written agenda for a meeting but you should consider having one when you can.

Because we have all attended meetings that have lulled us into a stupor, many of us groan at the very thought of attending yet another meeting. A memo or email invites us, and we dread the prospect of wasting our time. However, meetings can be important and valuable opportunities to share ideas. Meetings provide opportunities to clarify issues, to educate and to brainstorm. You and your colleagues can benefit from well-run meetings. Don't underestimate their value.

Well-run meetings usually have prepared agendas. What is an agenda? It is essentially a plan or road map for the meeting, consisting of a list of items in the order that they are to be discussed. Usually, these items are:

- The minutes or a recap of the previous meeting;
- A set of bullet point topics under 'old business';
- A set of bullet point topics under 'new business'.

Often it is useful to agree a tentative date for the next meeting as your last item before you adjourn. Most people will have diaries or smartphones to check their calendars and can record the date and time, thus saving you time and effort co-ordinating calendars at a later date.

The process of preparing an agenda involves you in thinking through the items in advance of the meeting and then prioritising them. And if you invite your colleagues to provide items for the agenda not only do you empower them, you also may learn about additional concerns you may have overlooked. Be sure to give them sufficient time and ask for their input by a certain date prior to the meeting.

Once you have put it together, send a copy of the agenda to the other attendees in advance of the meeting, to give them the opportunity to prepare. Because some of us need more reflective time than others, having the opportunity to consider the issues may improve the quality of the discussion. Individuals will have had time to think about questions or concerns and have supporting data to hand rather than having to respond spontaneously to a question like, "What's your reaction to the proposal?".

Some meetings may have only one item on the agenda; others have 20 or more. But when setting your agenda, be realistic. Think about whether one item might be so contentious or challenging that it could warrant an entire meeting or that attempting to discuss 20 items is unrealistic given the amount of time available. If a long list of items needs to be worked through, perhaps two shorter meetings would better than one long meeting. And if you have invited someone to speak, be sensitive to the amount of time you want to give them and how much time they may have to give you as well.

Because our minds wander, an agenda serves to rein us in and to stay focused – both before and during the meeting.


**See also**
**Q49**   How should I prepare for a formal meeting?
**Q51**   How important is the length and timing of a meeting?

## Q51    How important is the length and timing of a meeting?

Very. Research shows that adults need variety and can focus more effectively if meetings are no longer than 40 to 45 minutes. So try to keep your meetings within that length of time – if you can.

So, while we're used to being told that an upcoming meeting is "... on Friday at 9:00", or "... on Tuesday at 2:30", consider indicating the ending time, too. You could say that the meeting will be "an hour long", or that it "will run from 9:00 to 10:30", or that "it will not adjourn before noon". Having that information enables your colleagues to arrange their own schedules and to adjust their workloads.

Your meetings will be more productive if the participants aren't looking at their watches, stepping out to make phone calls and texts, or apologising for leaving early. When people are preoccupied with their own obligations, they have difficulty concentrating on the issues at hand. In addition, by giving them the approximate length of the meeting, they will appreciate your sensitivity to their workloads.

If you have a choice about the timing of a meeting, be aware of what day of the week or what time of the day is generally better for attendees in terms of convenience, productivity or effectiveness. First thing Monday morning may be best for workload, while Friday afternoon may be less productive.

One *caveat* about the length of meetings: if you call a 30-minute meeting or a 90-minute meeting, abide by that time. Keep an eye on the clock. People will value your consideration.

**See also**
**Q49**    How should I prepare for a formal meeting?
**Q50**    Why do I need a written agenda for a meeting?

## Q52    As chairperson, how should I manage a meeting?

If you called the meeting or are the chair, it is yours to run. You set the tone. You provide the right number of copies of material. You control discussions. If you don't, your meeting may get out of hand because some people like to hear the sound of their own voices, are oblivious to others' concerns, enjoy bringing in extraneous issues or are contentious by nature. Concentrate on the issues being discussed. When discussion becomes protracted, bring it back to the subject rather than let the talk wander far afield.

To maintain order or to rein in an enthusiastic participant, you can:
- Thank them for their enthusiasm and commitment;
- Point out that you all have a limited amount of time;
- Recommend that the new issues are important enough to raise at a subsequent meeting;
- Ask those concerned to provide the information and distribute it to the others present, then or at a future time.

In other words, without putting down individuals who tend toward lengthy explanations or presentations, stop them. The others present will be grateful – even if they don't say so. If you don't stop time-wasters, you will not meet your objectives for the meeting.

One way to lose support is to ask someone to take the time to prepare a report for a particular meeting and then to exclude it because the discussion of other issues has taken too long. How would you feel if you were that person, who put other tasks aside and rushed to meet a deadline? While you may offer an apology, you have set an unfortunate precedent.

To manage meetings better, ideally you should become familiar with *Robert's Rules of Order*. However, even if you are not using formal parliamentary rules, you need to control the process to ensure your meetings are successful.

**See also**

Q49   How should I prepare for a formal meeting?
Q53   As chairperson, how can I encourage participation at meetings?
Q62   What are my responsibilities as chairperson of a formal meeting?

## Q53    As chairperson, how can I encourage participation at meetings?

Time is an issue at most meetings, so it is important to stay on track. However, unless a meeting is purely informational, you want everyone to have a chance to offer their input or to ask questions, and some people are more diffident than others.

Certainly, you want to discourage individuals who use your meetings to discuss their own pet peeves or personal issues. With careful handling, such as "Thank you, let's make time to discuss this at the next meeting ...", you can control people who attempt to dominate discussions or who blurt out their opinions with complete disregard for someone else's desire to talk. But, while reining in those people, you also should encourage more reticent people to participate.

Be sensitive to the fact that not everyone thinks quickly or speaks comfortably at meetings. Some people are more reflective than others, are less willing to express their opinions or simply are shy. Being new to the organisation or to the issues may cause others to be reluctant to speak. The power structure may be a deterrent to others. Bullying or sarcastic behaviour may discourage still others. When you chair meetings, look around and become aware of who is participating and who is not. If the same person volunteers information or answers every question, invite comments from the quieter attendees. Ask direct questions, if necessary. While some people may be uncomfortable speaking, by asking them to join in, you are indicating that you value their insights.

Avoid using the technique of calling on each person in turn around the room or table. Knowing that their turn is coming, people may stop listening to others in order to prepare their own thoughts. They will not hear what the person two seats to the right has said. Then, having had their turn, they may relax and stop listening again because they are relieved that they are 'off the hook', or they may simply concede their opinion.

Your demeanour as the chair also encourages – or discourages – involvement. A smile, an acknowledgement, in the form of a quick "Thank you" makes a difference. If you become aware of others having side conversations, asking them to hold their thoughts while someone is speaking is always welcome.

Another method for encouraging involvement is to invite the participants to recommend items for the agenda in advance. People will feel a sense of ownership, and believe that their opinions are valued, because they have been asked to be part of the process. And they will be less likely to complain (or, at least, have less grounds for complaint) about the issues being discussed when they have been given the opportunity to offer suggestions and have declined to participate.

**See also**
**Q52**   As chairperson, how should I manage a meeting?

## Q54    Why should I prepare minutes of a meeting?

Meetings are valuable opportunities for sharing ideas. Too often, however, good ideas are praised at the time, but then forgotten. So as not to lose them, record key ideas, concerns and actions. While records are usually kept at formal meetings, not all meetings are formal. Nevertheless, it is important even in an informal setting to remember what has been said and by whom. For example, if someone volunteered to research an answer, to follow up on a question, to form a committee, or to report back at a subsequent meeting, those decisions should be recorded. If a brilliant notion is introduced, but there is no time for discussion, it would be a shame to forget the idea because no one had the foresight to take notes.

It doesn't matter whether you, a colleague or an assistant take the minutes, or record them for later transcription – someone should keep a record. Too many good ideas are lost because of the absence of minutes. Too many meetings rehash previously resolved issues because no one wrote down the agreed solutions at the time. And when there is no record, people may not be held accountable for their responsibilities.

Minutes should be written up quickly following a meeting. The longer they remain as notes, the more likely it is that the typed minutes will differ markedly from the original discussion, simply because memory fades.

**See also**

Q47    How can I get the best from an informal meeting?
Q48    How can I get the best from a formal meeting?
Q52    As chairperson, how should I manage a meeting?
Q70    What should I include in the minutes of meetings?

## Q55 How should I prepare to interview a candidate for a position in my organisation?

In addition to communicating over the phone or in writing, in business we also have to communicate in face-to-face interviews. We are interviewed for positions ourselves, we interview candidates and we provide supervisory, counselling or exit interviews.

Most job interviews cover similar ground. In one form or another, candidates are asked to describe their strengths and weaknesses. Or they might be asked to indicate what they are proudest of, or what they would change about themselves. Sometimes, candidates are asked why they should be hired or to describe the qualities they would bring to the position. Such questions should come as no surprise to candidates. Therefore, when you prepare for the interview, think how you get below the candidate's initial answers – think of some supplementary or follow-up questions to their likely answers.

If the candidate submitted a CV/resumé, covering letter or application form, have copies and reread them before you go to the interview to be sure you remember what they wrote. Also reread any job announcements or advertisements to recall exactly the language that was used to describe the position. This avoids wasting interview time covering information that's already known.

It is unusual for interviews to end without the candidate being given the opportunity to ask questions. Think through what a candidate might want to know about your organisation or the job – and prepare your answers.

When you are interviewing a candidate, you are determining not only whether they can do or learn to do the job, but also whether they can fit into your culture AND stay. Hiring and training is expensive, which is frequently why candidates are asked, "Why did you leave your last job?". By asking this, you are trying to determine what might make the person leave your organisation.

**See also**
**Q56** How can I improve as a recruitment interviewer?

## Q56    How can I improve as a recruitment interviewer?

One of the most common errors on the part of recruitment interviewers is to talk too much. The candidate for a job should do most of the talking. Your objective in the interview process is to learn as much as you can about them in a short time to determine whether they will fit into the job and into your organisation. Even with the inclusion of assessments and personality testing, interviewing is not a scientific process. And even though the role of 'intuition' is under the microscope, sometimes it is a feeling or a gut reaction that gives you a signal.

You know that a wrong hiring decision can be costly. The person you hire will be on a learning curve and thus unable to give you 100% from their day one. To bring people up to speed, you train and you mentor. So, if you hire someone who leaves after six months, you will have made a costly hiring decision. Then, if you decide to refill the vacancy, you have to go through the interview process again, the hiring and the training – with no greater guarantee of success. And you probably have other responsibilities to be fulfilled during your working day.

So, the more you know about candidates the better. The more talking they do, the more you will learn about them. Therefore, unless you have the time to schedule multiple interviews for each candidate:

- Avoid spending excessive time describing the organisation and yourself – send them this information in a note before the interview;
- Avoid asking questions that can be answered with only a 'yes' or 'no'; instead, ask open-ended questions that require the candidates to talk more freely;
- Actively listen to what they say;
- Ask follow-up questions like "Why …?" and "How …?" or "Can you give an example?" to elicit more information;
- Ask them to solve mini-cases by asking, "How would you handle …?";

- Ask them to defend their positions when challenged, by playing devil's advocate.

In other words, use the opportunity to learn as much as you can about the candidate by preparing good questions and by withholding reports of your own adventures. Your goal is to hear what the candidates have to say.

**See also**
**Q57**    Should I prepare questions or just chat with a candidate?

## Q57    Should I prepare questions or just chat with a candidate?

While you may have a chat with a candidate over lunch, dinner or coffee, which may elicit more surprising answers, for a formal interview prepare your questions in advance. Doing so enables you to think hard about the nature of the position that you want to fill and the kind of person you need to handle those responsibilities. And it eliminates the burden of having to make up questions on the spot.

If you are a member of an interview panel, work with your colleagues in developing a set of questions. This will avoid overlap and allow you to decide in advance who will ask which questions.

If you are seeing multiple candidates, it is best to ask each one the same questions – for example, about strengths and weaknesses, background, five-year plans and the critical "Why did you leave your last job?". Also ask questions specific to the position or to the organisation.

Of course, follow-up questions depend on the candidates' responses, but only ask questions that help you understand their suitability for the position on offer – not just those that satisfy your curiosity!

Developing good questions takes time. It is easier to prepare them in advance. The professionalism and preparedness with which you greet the candidate will form a lasting impression about you and your organisation. Even if you turn the candidate down for the position, you want them to think well of the experience because in the future they may have need of your products or your services or be willing to recommend your organisation to someone who does.

**See also**
**Q56**    How can I improve as a recruitment interviewer?

## Q58    How should I prepare for a job interview myself?

Suppose you are the candidate either for a prospective position external to your own company or for an internal transfer or promotion, and you have been invited to an interview. You want the job. So, how do you prepare? First and foremost, do your homework.

### Research
This involves learning about the industry and the organisation, which may whet or dampen your desire to work for the organisation. Knowing that the organisation has been undergoing a major organisational change, recently has launched a new product or is closing some of its branches will enable you to answer the interviewer's questions and to ask your own. At the interview, if you are knowledgeable about the organisation, you will communicate that you want to be perceived as a serious candidate.

If the interview is for an internal transfer or promotion, you may have a good sense of the organisation already, but you still may want to get a sense of the bigger picture, and of why the position is open. One *caveat*: be supportive of other candidates, even though you are in competition with them. When the interviews are done, you may be working for one of them or they may be working for you – either way, it's better that you have a good starting relationship.

If the position is with another organisation, then:

- Go to the library or online and read annual reports and business journal articles about the organisation and its people;
- Check the company's website;
- Request copies of current corporate literature, if this is made publicly available;
- Become aware of what is happening in the world in general, with the organisation specifically and with other organisations in the same or similar sectors;

- Pay attention to the news;
- Pay attention to changing markets;
- Find people who might know the company -- people who are doing business with the organisation or working for them. Talk to them and ask questions about their experiences.

**At the interview**
Most job interviews cover similar ground. In one form or another, candidates are asked to describe their strengths and weaknesses. Or they might be asked to indicate what they are proudest of, or what they would change about themselves. Sometimes, candidates are asked why they should be hired or to describe the qualities they would bring to the position. If you are the candidate, such questions should come as no surprise. Therefore, when you prepare for the interview, think how you are going to respond to them. Be ready with answers based on your education and experience, both paid and unpaid, which appear on your CV/resumé. Many people forget that being in a club or on a team or volunteering often involves transferable skills. Perhaps you had to lead, or organise or arrange or convince or sell.

If you submitted a CV/resumé, covering letter or application form, reread a copy before you go to the interview to be sure you remember what you wrote. Also reread any job announcements or advertisements to recall exactly the language that was used to describe the position. By doing so, you should be able to anticipate some of the questions. For example, suppose the description says that the company is looking for someone who is detail-oriented. Be ready with examples from your experience to demonstrate your attention to detail.

Arrive at the interview prepared with questions about the position and the organisation. But remember: a first interview is not about salary and benefits. Of course, you want to earn a living, but only when you are sure that you can or want to do the job, will be taught how to perform your duties and will fit into the culture should you discuss money and benefits. Initially you are interviewing with the organisation to determine whether you can and want to work with them. Even in a brutal job market, you don't want to feel miserably out of place. If you are happier working with technology rather than with people, a position involving 90% customer service work may not be for you.

At the same time and in the same way, the people who are interviewing you are determining whether you can do or learn to do the job, fit into their culture AND stay. Hiring and training is expensive. Organisations want to have a strong sense that you will remain with them, which is frequently why candidates are asked, "Why did you leave your last job?". The interviewer is trying to determine what might make you leave the organisation – be sure to reassure them.

### See also
**Q59** What questions should I ask if I am a candidate for a position?
**Q60** What kind of personal examples should I offer in a job interview?

## Q59     What questions should I ask if I am a candidate for a position?

It is unusual for interviews to end without an opportunity for you to ask questions. Something may have been said in passing about reorganising a department or about other changes in the organisation, which should prompt you to want to know more about the implications. You might want to ask why the position is open, to whom the position reports or what training is provided. So, when you are asked, "Do you have questions?", some may naturally arise from what has been said during the course of the interview.

But you need to ask something. By doing so, you are demonstrating that you have invested time to learn about the organisation and are aware of changes that may be occurring or that may affect it.

In addition, design your questions so that you can determine whether you will fit the organisation, whether your talents will be used or underused or whether you will be asked to do the work of three people because of cutbacks. Interviews go both ways.

**See also**
**Q58**    How should I prepare for a job interview myself?
**Q60**    What kind of personal examples should I offer in a job interview?

## Q60 What kind of personal examples should I offer in a job interview?

If you are an architect or graphic designer or model, it is easy to bring your portfolio with you to show the interviewer(s) the quality of your work.

But suppose interviewers are looking for intangibles. The job description called for someone who was bright, energetic and good with people, and you have told the interviewers that you are. You need to be ready with evidence to prove it. The best way is to think about what activities you have done in the past and come armed with examples to demonstrate that you are as you describe yourself. Recall situations from your life experience that illustrate those qualities. Refer to those experiences during your interview: "When I was a shop assistant over the Christmas holidays, I had to deal with people under stress from the holidays" or "As assistant manager, I frequently was asked to ...". If you are changing fields, show how your abilities and skills transfer to the new position.

And remember, your experience need not be from a paid position. For example, being able to motivate people on your school athletic team should translate into being able to motivate others in an office. Value those experiences and offer them, rather than censoring them because you feel they are not relevant.

**See also**
**Q58** How should I prepare for a job interview myself?
**Q59** What questions should I ask if I am a candidate for a position?

## Q61    What if something goes wrong with a meeting?

Lots can go wrong with meetings. Despite your best efforts:

- A broken elevator or traffic snarl-up may cause you or other attendees to arrive late;
- Mobile phones may ring or vibrate noisily;
- Computer technology may let you down;
- The airconditioning may refuse to cool when it's sweltering or heat when it's freezing cold.

When organising meetings, all you can do is to anticipate problems, plan alternative solutions and stand ready to implement those alternatives speedily when necessary.

However, more often than not the problem with meetings is due to human rather than technological issues. Bluntly, most meetings are badly managed.

As the organiser, you have decided who is invited to the meeting. Use that foreknowledge to prepare for participants' behaviour and to prevent one participant from venting their frustration, another from constantly interrupting or a third from trying to dominate every discussion.

It is the chair's responsibility to conduct the meeting. Just as a conductor manages the orchestra, encouraging and discouraging certain musicians at different times, so too you may have to ask that everyone stay focused on the issues or hold their opinions until all the facts are known, or allow someone to finish, or encourage the more reticent to speak.

**See also**
**Q49**    How should I prepare for a formal meeting?
**Q52**    As chairperson, how should I manage a meeting?

## Q62 What are my responsibilities as chairperson of a formal meeting?

As chairperson, your key responsibility is for time management. You are responsible for managing the entire proceedings: from calling the meeting to order and starting it on time, through ensuring that all the topics are given appropriately-balanced time for discussion, to adjourning the meeting with an indication of when the next meeting will take place or an action plan will be presented.

To limit problems:

- Distribute a written agenda in advance, showing the topics for discussion;
- Plan how to allocate time between topics, allowing some slack – then stick to this timing;
- Defer tangential issues to the end of the meeting or a future meeting;
- Discourage garrulous attendees from dominating the proceedings;
- Encourage diffident attendees to participate;
- Ban side conversations – only one person should be speaking at any time;
- Manage the discussion to keep broadly to your time-plan – if discussion on a topic, threatens to overrun, decide whether to flex your time-plan by allowing more time for this topic at the expense of another or to halt discussion and defer it to a future meeting;
- Respect questioners and repeat their questions, if necessary, so that everyone hears and understands their point;
- Ensure that everyone can hear whoever is speaking – use microphones if necessary;
- At the end, take a few minutes to summarise the discussions, highlighting what has been agreed and allocating actions to participants as appropriate. Also give an indication of when minutes of the meeting will be made available.

**See also**

Q50    Why do I need a written agenda for a meeting?
Q51    How important is the length and timing of a meeting?
Q52    As chairperson, how should I manage a meeting?

# WRITING – OFFLINE & ONLINE

## Q63    What types of writing do I need to master?

In your role as a businessperson, you are likely to write a wide range of documents, including:

- Emails;
- Funding applications;
- Letters;
- Minutes of meetings;
- Newsletter articles;
- Notes- to yourself, to others or for filing;
- Press releases;
- Proposals;
- Reports.

Each of these is different and requires a slightly different approach.

**See also**
**Q64**    Why is time important when writing?
**Q65**    How does the written word differ from the spoken word?
**Q66**    Why do I need to think about specific readers when writing?
**Q99**    How can I develop my writing skills?

# Q64 Why is time important when writing?

Writing for business always should be clear and to the point. It is not intended for entertainment or for a poetic turn of phrase – for that, read Seamus Heaney, John Grisham or Maeve Binchy. Business writing should communicate ideas clearly and succinctly to ensure success.

Writing takes time. One reason so much of business writing is not as good as it could be is because we do not dedicate enough time to it. Much of what we write is completed under pressure. While we may produce good work, we don't always take the time to produce superior work. Too often, when we write memos, reports, letters or emails, we distribute or send what are, in fact, drafts. We rarely build time into our days to reread or rewrite what we have written to ensure that our words accurately and clearly convey our messages. Instead, we work to the deadline and move on immediately to the next task.

Think about how you write. Do you plan blocks of time for writing, or do you fit it in between other activities? Look at your diary or organiser. Do you have specific times for writing? We record times for appointments, meetings or phone calls. So, why can't we make time for writing? After your 9:00 conference call, your 11:00 meeting, make a slot – say from 11:30 for an hour – to draft your speech or write your proposal.

Note that good writing always requires rewriting. So always plan some time to review and rewrite important documents. Give your draft a few hours, overnight or a few days to sit. Then reread what you have written. Is it logical? Is it clear? Have you used the best words? Build rewriting into your calendar.

Clarity in writing facilitates the work of others and minimises the time that you spend explaining what you meant. That extra rewrite will make a difference in the reactions and responses that you get.

**See also**
Q2   Why is clarity essential for effective communication?
Q67   What should I look for when I reread my work?

## Q65    How does the written word differ from the spoken word?

Writing is usually a solitary experience. You write in quiet, at home, in your cubicles, in an airport lounge, on a train or in your offices. While you may be alone with your own thoughts, never forget that you are writing for an audience.

When you speak face-to-face, you can see your listener. You know whether you are speaking to a man or a woman – and how old they are. You can learn quickly what their native tongue might be. You can gauge their frame of mind at that moment. You can judge your audience's mood and/or their feelings toward you or about what you are saying. Because you can do so, you can make adjustments to your communication. You can speak louder or softer; you can alter your own body language; you can smile or pause or soften your tone; or you can ask a question. If you see a quizzical look, you can ask whether you need to repeat something that you have just said; if you see a bored reaction, you may want to speed up or cut.

However, when you write, that reaction may be days away, or it may never come at all. The reader is not physically there with you. He or she could be in the next room or miles away. Wherever they are, they are unable to ask what you meant by that last sentence or by the previous paragraph. So, you cannot immediately gauge reaction and modify what you are trying to communicate.

Therefore, when you put pen to paper or finger to keyboard, keep the reader in your mind. Imagine those people. Think about what they know, what they don't know and what they need to know to understand what you are writing. Therefore, every word, every sentence, every paragraph needs to be thought through with the reader in mind.

### See also
**Q19**    What should I learn about my audience?
**Q66**    Why do I need to think about specific readers when writing?

# Q66 Why do I need to think about specific readers when writing?

Although a talk might be filmed or recorded, most are not. But writing is almost always an indelible and permanent record. After the fact, you can't say, "Oops, I didn't mean to write that", or "Disregard page 4".

Because of this, think not only about the audience in general but also about specific readers. Be sure that you haven't written anything that might be misconstrued or faults someone. If uncensored words fall into the wrong hands, ask yourself who might be surprised, offended or angered. What's your relationship with that person? Will you lose credibility? Think about the implications, when you distribute your writing.

And be sure you know the distribution. Don't exclude anyone. When distributing written work, it is easy to hurt or anger people by forgetting to give them a copy and to bewilder others by including them when they shouldn't be.

Be particularly careful with email. It's easy to send an email to the wrong recipient(s). So take a moment to check before you hit the 'send' button.

**See also**
**Q19** What should I learn about my audience?

## Q67    What should I look for when I reread my work?

In addition to being sensitive to the human implications of your written work, consider the technical aspects, too. Edit your work. Rough drafts are just that — rough. They are the thoughts that you have rapidly put down on paper.

Editing is refining your work to ensure that your message is clear. When you edit:

- **Check for inconsistencies:** Be sure that what you say on page 1 of a report is consistent with what you say on page 49. Be sure that the precise language of a problem statement or research questions remains unchanged as the number of pages increases;

- **Link ideas:** To help readers follow your thinking, give signals to them by writing introductory paragraphs and introductory sentences. An introductory paragraph states your purpose and describes what the reader should expect to read and in what order. Each paragraph should follow the previous one logically. When you edit, use words to link paragraphs, such as, 'first', 'second', or 'third', or, 'therefore', or 'as a consequence'. These link ideas and make your thoughts easier to follow;

- **Write with nouns and verbs:** Effective business writing is to the point. Dickensian or Joycean sentences are not appropriate in business. Write in sentences that are short and simple. Don't overload them with descriptive words, clauses and phrases. The additional verbiage makes it difficult for the reader to find the noun and the verb and thus to decipher your meaning;

- **Eliminate qualifiers:** Qualifiers are words like 'rarely', 'sort of', 'kind of', 'rather'. They make your writing vague. Relying on words like 'sort of' suggests that you didn't have time to find the right ones initially. For example, she was 'sort of pretty'. Well, was she pretty, stunning, elegant, cute, sensuous or attractive? Eliminate qualifiers and find the words that say what you mean;

- **Avoid negative expressions:** Remember taking exams with questions that began "Which one of these is not ...?" Those questions usually took longer to answer because you had to be sure that you interpreted them correctly. If you use the positive rather than the negative, it is easier for the reader to interpret your message;

- **Beware of ambiguity:** In a draft, you need not be concerned with words like 'its', 'them', 'that', 'their', 'this' and 'those'. But be sure to correct them in your final version. Be sure the reader can determine what those pronouns refer to in your sentence. "We gave the products to the women. They were excellent." What was 'excellent'? The products? Or the women?

- **Keep it simple:** Your writing should be clear and uncluttered. Make lists. Use bullet points. Create headings. Tell the reader that a list will follow; then provide the list. Eliminate tangential information and unnecessary repetition. Remove material that doesn't support your argument. Use words that are easily understood. A 'house' does not need to be an 'abode' or a 'fire' a 'conflagration' just because you are writing a formal report. Keep your words and sentence structure simple;

- **Check for spelling, grammatical and arithmetical errors:** While your wordprocessing software can check spelling for you, don't rely on it to the exclusion of your own editing. Double-check 'it's' and 'its'; 'their', 'there' and 'they're'; 'your and 'you're'. Be sure that plural nouns have plural verbs.

In essence, when you reread, check for clarity and correctness. Be sure that paragraphs haven't been omitted or sentences misplaced. Check to see that numbers add up, that capital letters are used when appropriate, that abbreviations are correct and that punctuation is accurate.

**See also**

Q2    Why is clarity essential for effective communication?
Q65   How does the written word differ from the spoken word?

## Q68 What are the basic formats of memos and letters?

We spend many hours writing emails, memos and/or letters. These are short pieces of communication, so brief that we often jot down information quickly. Be careful. Less formal documents should be written as carefully as your longer more formal work.

Whether you are writing a letter or a memo, decide how you want it to look on the page. Most memos begin with:

**To:**

**From:**

**Date:** ___

**Subject:**

Sometimes the word 'reference' is used instead of 'subject'. Headings enable the reader to know immediately who sent the memo and what it is about. The date provides you with a record and enables you to track a conversation or discussion of an issue, thus, enabling you to see the sequence of decision-making. Because the memo format is familiar to most people, there is no need to write 'Memo' at the top of the page. If you are sending hard copies, your initials next to your name are sufficient rather than a signature.

Letters have a format, too. If you use company letterhead paper, then you don't have to include the address. If you don't use letterhead, write your mailing address on the upper right corner of the page. Below, on the left side, write the address of the person to whom the letter is being sent:

> Mr. John Jones, Secretary
> Whatsis Ltd
> 50 High Street
> West Billingsford
> London WX1 2YZ

Then leave a few lines, and add the date.

Next, after a few more lines spaces, write:

Dear Mr. Jones,

And then begin your letter to Mr. Jones.

Even though the letter is addressed to Mr. Jones, it's remarkable how often people write 'Dear Sir' for the salutation. Instead, write, 'Dear Mr. Jones'.

In both letters and memos, your first paragraph following the salutation should introduce the subject, the middle one or two or three paragraphs should develop your ideas and the final paragraph should state the conclusion, restate your point or call for action.

Letters typically close with 'Yours sincerely' or 'Sincerely yours' followed by your name. Unlike memos, letters are signed with your full name.

There are endless variations on memos and letters in terms of style and placement, so consider encouraging the use of a 'house style'. Having a consistent format projects a professional image for you, your office and your organisation. It suggests an attention to detail, which your audience may appreciate.

And a brief note about email subject lines. When you send emails, ensure the subject line refers specifically to the content. Frequently with a string of emails, the content diverges from the original subject – just as in a conversation – but the same subject line remains, making it difficult to tell at a quick glance what the email refers to. Clear subject lines also help the reader to know which of their many emails to open first.

**See also**
**Q69** How is writing an email different from writing a letter or memo?

## Q69    How is writing an email different from writing a letter or memo?

By and large, emails tend to be read on screen. True, some people still print them out, but in most cases, they are read on PCs, laptops or smartphones. And in today's world, businesspeople can receive hundreds of e-mails a day – not including 'spam' or newsletters.

Because of their volume and the speed with which they are read or not read, and the ease with which they can be overlooked and deleted, it is important that what you write on the subject line is carefully thought out.

While it's convenient to use the 'Reply' button, avoid using the same subject line for several e-mails, weeks apart, on different topics. So, if your thread of emails starts with 'upgrading the web site', don't allow later emails to shift to scheduling a meeting without changing the subject line and starting a new thread. Otherwise, your readers may skip the email because they think they are done with the upgrading issue.

Next, ensure that your e-mail is as succinct as possible. Use numbered points rather than narrative; this will help you to summarise your thoughts and make them easier for the reader to understand. Make clear to the reader what you want them to do after reading your email: "Please confirm that you will deliver our order no later than 6 pm on Friday, 27 October" or "Can you check when Joe is available for a meeting next week?".

Because of the volume of email that people receive today, they may rush over important information you wish them to have. So help them to make wise decisions by making your email easy to read and understand.

**See also**
**Q65**    How does the written word differ from the spoken word?
**Q68**    What are the basic formats of memos and letters?

## Q70 What should I include in the minutes of meetings?

As you know, keeping minutes allows you to keep track of what has occurred at meetings. Because our days are filled with myriad interactions, it is easy to forget who promised to do what or was asked to follow through on a task, so keeping track of decisions or action points made at meetings is essential and valuable.

When you write up minutes of a meeting, unless there are serious legal or contractual concerns, there is no need to include or transcribe the entire discussion that surrounded an issue. While you may have jotted some notes, your written minutes can simply be a record of the decisions taken and the allocation of follow-up actions. While there may have been a lengthy discussion about the formation of a committee or of the delegation of an assignment, your minutes simply should indicate the result.

If you are using parliamentary procedure to run a more formal meeting, then your minutes may include more details about who 'moved the question' or called for a vote and the outcome of that vote. If you have a note that John agreed (or was delegated) to set up a committee and report back at the June meeting, that bit of information reminds you that John's report needs to be an item on the June agenda.

Clearly, formal committee and board meetings should be minuted. But it's often useful, immediately after an informal meeting, to note down decisions and action points. If you circulate your note to the other people at the meeting, rather than say "Please find attached minutes of our meeting …", you could say "I thought it might be helpful to note what we agreed this morning – see below".

**See also**
**Q54** Why should I prepare minutes of a meeting?

## Q71    How should I structure a formal report?

Reports can be overwhelming – both for you to write and for your audience to read. Writing reports involves thinking and planning. Well-organised, clearly-written reports are helpful for readers whether they are accident reports, feasibility studies, progress reports, or status reports.

The classic structure for a formal written report usually includes:

- **The title page:** This includes the name of the report, the author and the date (and perhaps a version number if there are several drafts);

- **The table of contents:** This is a listing of the sections and their page numbers;

- **The introduction:** This section includes the terms of reference, a description of the method used in assembling the data and the scope or limitations of the document. It is usually no more than a few pages long;

- **The findings:** This section includes the facts. It consists of the raw data essential to the study including statistical data, answers to questions, detailed descriptions, numbers, or quotations from interviews. This is the main body of the report;

- **The conclusions:** These are your interpretations of the data analysed in the findings section. The conclusions should be consistent with the purpose of your report;

- **The recommendations:** These are suggestions based on your conclusions. Sometimes, for the convenience of readers, the recommendations also are summarised in the Introduction;

- **The appendices:** These are the sections at the end of the report that include letters, diagrams, tables and other raw data. Putting such material in one section at the end rather than throughout the document is less disruptive to your readers.

Not every report has all these sections, but this is the order in which reports typically are organised.

**See also**

**Q72**    What makes a good title for a report?

**Q73**    How can I help my reader understand complex material?

**Q74**    Can I put my opinions in a report?

# Q72    What makes a good title for a report?

Business writing calls for different titles than the latest Ken Bruen or James Patterson blockbuster that the publisher wants you to grab off the shelf or download to your ebook reader. Titles on reports, whether formal or informal, need to precisely reflect the content. Take your time when choosing a title: it's what people see first.

Often titles for reports are too short or inaccurate, when they should help the reader determine what is inside the document. Suppose you write a report and title it 'Mexico'. With such an all-encompassing title, readers could reasonably expect to learn about some or all of the food, resorts, climate, flora, fauna, currency, government, history, weather or economy of Mexico. But if your report is about the economic effects of Hurricane Pauline on the tourism market in Cancun, Mexico in 1998, then title your report just that.

Some people choose to use an attention-grabbing title and then add a subtitle to expand the notion or to clarify – for example, you might title your report 'Mexico', clarifying the topic in a subtitle, 'An analysis of the implications of climate change on the peso'.

The process for arriving at a title involves narrowing and narrowing your draft title until it relates exactly to the core of your subject matter. Asking "So what?" or "What about the subject?" should lead you to a title that suggests the value or importance of your topic to your readers.

**See also**
Q71    How should I structure a formal report?
Q73    How can I help my reader understand complex material?
Q74    Can I put my opinions in a report?

## Q73    How can I help my reader understand complex material?

Developing an outline helps you and your reader to see natural divisions in your material.

Suppose you have three sections in your report: introduction, findings and conclusions. As you are analysing your data, however, you realise that your findings section can be broken into different categories. Suppose you interviewed people who eat in the company restaurant for breakfast, for lunch, and for coffee breaks. You might decide that you can make three sub-divisions in the findings, broken down by each of the three meals, the time of the day or the nature of the purchases. Thus you might divide the findings section into three sections: A, B and C.

As a report becomes more complex, it may begin to look like this:

**II Findings**

    A Breakfast

        1 Beverages

           1a

           1b

    B Lunch

    C Coffee Breaks

**III Conclusions**

**IV Recommendations**

Some people prefer not to use roman numerals, so they might have sections 1, 2, and 3 with 1.1, 2.1 and 3.1 as subheads. Regardless of the method you select, essentially you are breaking up the material so that like is together with like and any supporting arguments are placed with the item to be defended or presented.

In fact, creating a structure helps you in thinking through your own material as well as assisting you in presenting it to your audience so that they readily follow your logic or your argument.

**See also**
**Q71**   How should I structure a formal report?
**Q72**   What makes a good title for a report?
**Q74**   Can I put my opinions in a report?

## Q74    Can I put my opinions in a report?

In writing a report, your opinions, which are based on your conclusions, typically appear in the recommendations section only. They must be substantiated views, supported by data, by facts.

And you should only offer your opinions when asked for them.

For example, suppose you are writing a report on an accident involving an employee named Sally. In your gut, you suspect that Sally herself caused the accident because of her own carelessness. But, unless you can substantiate your views, you cannot say so. Your report should record only what happened on the day of the accident.

As you assemble the data, you may learn from an unimpeachable source that Sally is a frequent victim of accidents. Once you verify that information, you may want to write a subsequent report (or add to your report, if you have not yet completed it) listing the dates of previous accidents as well as the nature of those accidents – again, you report only the facts. If you also discover that Sally is the only person in the organisation who has ever been involved in such accidents, you can **conclude** that no one else has had any accidents. Therefore, you might **recommend** that she be given additional training to avoid the problem in future or that she be transferred to a department where she is not likely to be exposed to risk of additional accidents. Your conclusions follow from the facts – and your recommendations (your opinion) from your conclusions.

You should not make recommendations in your report if your purpose was simply to record what happened at a specific time on a specific day. Even if it is your gut instinct, you cannot characterise Sally as 'sloppy' or 'lazy', nor can you discuss other accidents in which she may have been involved. That experience on that day is the only subject, and requires factual reporting.

**See also**
**Q71**    How should I structure a formal report?
**Q72**    What makes a good title for a report?

**Q73**  How can I help my reader understand complex material?

**Q75**  What is the difference between a recommendation and a conclusion?

## Q75 What is the difference between a recommendation and a conclusion?

Be sure you know the difference between a recommendation and a conclusion. To clarify, consider a colleague, Mary. She says that she feels warm, complains of a headache, feels faint and looks pale. What conclusion can you draw?

Based on the facts you have, you can **conclude** only that she is unwell — not much more. You do not have enough information to conclude whether she has the plague, pneumonia, influenza or is pregnant – or any of these.

Having concluded that she is unwell, then you can **recommend** a course of action for her. You might suggest that she lie down, go to the nurse or doctor or take an aspirin, but again you cannot do much more. You do not have enough data to suggest that she be quarantined or to buy cigars to celebrate the impending birth of a child. If you do, then you are generalising beyond your data.

Again, you might have noticed groups of people standing around the photocopier. You might assume that they are socialising and be annoyed that they are not at their desks. Or you might assume that the copier is unable to handle the volume of work. But before making a recommendation either to buy a new copier or to encourage people to chat in the coffee area, you need to collect more data to turn either of those two assumptions into a conclusion.

If you research the issue, you might discover that the toner needs to be replaced frequently and causes delays because you have no spare cartridges on hand. Or you might determine that some people are less proficient with all the options on the copier, and that they cause delays for other users. Either way, your recommendation will be quite different. In one instance, you might want to have more toner on hand; in the other, you may recommend a brief training session to introduce people to the functions of this particular photocopier, or post a bulletin, or provide an instruction sheet.

In other words, when you make your recommendations about business decisions, be sure that you are drawing conclusions based on facts and not on suppositions. Then, and only then, can you make sound recommendations. Your reports always should make that distinction.

**See also**
**Q33**    What's the risk in over-generalising?
**Q74**    Can I put my opinions in a report?

## Q76 What should I consider when developing visuals?

Your artwork is intended to support your message, so it is essential that your audience be able to interpret your design. Can they see the detail clearly? Can they decipher it? Can they relate the image(s) to your words? Suppose your visual is a blueprint or x-ray, are you sure that everyone seeing it knows how to read it?

To help you, think about your reaction to websites you visit. Think about them and compare them. You know immediately which ones are user-friendly and which ones are not. You know which ones you like and which ones you don't. Some are clear; others are confusing. Some use faint type, others use too much bold type with indecipherable images and are too cluttered. Some have too many links and others have too few. Some require you to think too much or to take multiple steps to get where you want to go. In essence, what works for you on websites, you might consider when you develop your own visuals.

Consider colour combinations. While green and blue may look pretty and softer, black on white is easier to read. While block lettering may look imposing, the combination of upper and lower case is easier to decipher.

Be sure that you test your visual by projecting it on a wall or screen. Too often, they don't fit. The bottom or top may be cut off, or the colour you chose that looks beautiful at two inches is washed out at 15 feet. The font size may be too small or overwhelming. Design with the venue and audience in mind.

### See also
Q28  What should I consider when I use images?
Q77  Why are titles essential for charts and graphs?
Q78  How can I make a slide more effective?
Q79  How should I use charts and visuals in a report?

## Q77 Why are titles essential for charts and graphs?

Graphs and charts need titles. The audience needs to be told what they are reading or seeing. We cannot concentrate indefinitely on what we are reading or hearing because our minds are active, and we are thinking about our immediate feelings, of hunger, or aches and pains, of reports or chores to do, of having the car serviced, of posting a letter, or of remembering someone's birthday or anniversary. So think of titles as signposts to keep the audience on the path with you.

Remember too that interruptions occur. People arrive late and miss the introduction to your talk, or they may suddenly be called away or have to take a call or rush to a meeting. And in the case of reports, it is unusual for people to be able to read long reports in one sitting, so you need to help them return to where they left off with ease.

In a presentation, if you are using multiple images, putting a title above or below each image helps the audience stay focused and follow your logic. In this way, with your help, they are reminded of the relationship of the slide to the points you are making verbally. In written reports, be sure to label charts and graphs as well and to refer to the title in the text. Typically we write, "Table 2 on page 2 compares apples to oranges" – this both directs the reader to the table and tells them what to expect from it.

**See also**
**Q76** What should I consider when developing visuals?
**Q78** How can I make a slide more effective?
**Q79** How should I use charts and visuals in a report?

## Q78    How can I make a slide more effective?

Simple is better. Less is more. Using websites as a frame of reference, think about some that you have seen. Some are cluttered with links, narrative, images, and pop-ups, which may be off-putting. If there is too much to see on a page, your eyes may wander up and down, or left and right, and you wonder where to start reading. And too much effort becomes distracting. Therefore, it is easier for the reader to follow the flow of your narrative, if you keep your images simple.

If you want people to recall your image because it is important, be sure that it is not buried in too much detail, too many lines, or bullet points, bars or numbers. Financial reports, in particular, need to be simplified for visual presentation. Pie charts and bar graphs help, but not one in which the viewer is unable to decipher the numbers, the percentages or the dates. If all the material is essential, then consider dividing the data into multiple visuals rather than trying to develop one all-encompassing chart on a single slide.

When you are presenting, it is wiser to have no more than three bullet points on a slide, otherwise not only will your image be cluttered, you will have to use a smaller font, and most important, you risk your audience jumping ahead and reading all the bullets while you are still addressing the first one. This is why some presenters opt to show one slide with one bullet, then have a slide with bullets one and two, then another slide with bullets one, two and three.

In addition, your bullets need only be phrases – not full sentences. And when you create your bullets, be consistent. Try to have each bullet begin with the same part of speech. For example:

- Eat
- Drink and
- Be merry.

These three bullet points are all verbs. Look how much easier it is to read and remember them than three bullets that say:

- Eat

- Considering drinking, and
- The art of being merry.

**See also**
**Q76**  What should I consider when developing visuals?
**Q77**  Why are titles essential for charts and graphs?
**Q79**  How should I use charts and visuals in a report?

## Q79    How should I use charts and visuals in a report?

Charts and visuals are used to clarify or to substantiate what you are explaining or recommending. They can appear in an appendix, or they can be placed in the body of the work. It is always your decision. First, ask yourself, do these illustrations enhance the argument or clarify the issues? If I use a chart, will my discussion be easier to understand than if I use a narrative paragraph? If yes, then ask how much of the data do you need to make your point. You may not need every page of the statistical analysis.

Let's suppose you developed a questionnaire or survey. Is it critical to interrupt the flow to include the entire survey starting on page 7 of your report? Would it be better to indicate that the survey appears in Appendix A? Please note, you should tell the reader exactly where to find it in the report. What you don't want is to have them flipping back and forth through unnumbered pages or untitled sections in search of your survey.

If you think it is important to include one question from the survey in the narrative, then do so. Avoid asking the reader to go to the back of the document to find the question. Again, you want to make it easier, not more complicated. You might write "Question 12 of the survey asked, '...'". Be sure that the wording in the question from the survey is exactly the same as what you have written in the narrative. Don't paraphrase.

That point is true of charts and visuals. Make up clear titles which you number or put letters on: Chart one, two, three, or A or B or C, etc. As you write, make specific reference to the one you want the reader to look at writing, see Chart A on page 6, or see Chart 1 below. If possible have the chart as close to the reference as possible. Again, you want to avoid having the reader flip through the pages to find the chart.

With regard to the chart itself, include only what is essential and eliminate what is extraneous. Direct the reader to that line or set of figures or percentages that you want them to see. It might read something like, "...as indicated on Chart 3, page 6, the percentage for 2010 was less than 2011."

**See also**
**Q76**    What should I consider when developing visuals?
**Q77**    Why are titles essential for charts and graphs?
**Q78**    How can I make a slide more effective?

## Q80 How should I acknowledge other people's contribution to a report?

First, it is critical that you acknowledge other people's contribution to your work. It is the sign of a professional. At the very least, it is good manners; at the extreme, it may clear you from charges of plagiarism.

Most of what we do involves a team. In writing a book, other people may have done the research, provided guidance, given time for interviews or offered insights. In a formal document, you can list the contributors, indicating the role they played, or you can write a paragraph identifying by whom and how you were assisted, or you can state in the *Introduction* that "John Smith designed the survey". Whether this appears at the start or end of the report is your choice, but the acknowledgement should be there in some form.

And if you quote something that someone else has said, you should indicate who said it – and in what context.

Understandably, people become disaffected when their input is not acknowledged. It takes very little effort to recognise other people's work where it has contributed to your own.

**See also**

**Q3** How does being an effective communicator affect my personal credibility and professionalism?

## Q81    What must I beware of when using social media for my organisation?

You need to be aware that social media is both 'social' and 'media'. More important, it is both immediate and permanent.

If you write on your Facebook page that you are "sick and tired of client X", someone is going to see it and someone is likely to react.

Be careful. Before posting photographs from the office party or writing a comment on a blog or social media site, take a moment and think of the implications. How does what you post make you – and others – look? Have you created a potential legal or ethical problem? Run the notion or image by someone else.

Never have we had to be as politically aware as we are now. Be it a misspelled word, poor grammar, awkward sentence structure, a view on a social issue, a political stance, with a click or the press of a button, that view is shared and interpreted and examined. Tread carefully, as once posted, your comments or images can be shared worldwide – and are difficult to remove.

It may be necessary to introduce a policy that all posts to social media sites must be approved – by a head of department, the organisation's PR adviser or whoever. Sure, this will kill spontaneity – but a lawsuit could kill you or your organisation too.

**See also**
**QUICK WIN SOCIAL MEDIA MARKETING**

# SPEAKING & PRESENTING

## Q82 What should I look for when I visit the venue in advance of my talk?

Talking one-to-one in business with someone is an everyday occurrence. Speaking to groups is a less frequent experience and thus more daunting for most of us. You may feel alone and vulnerable. No matter how well prepared you are, most of us always have a nagging sense that disaster may befall us or that we may make a fool of ourselves. One of the easiest and quickest ways to gain confidence is by taking a few minutes – literally a few minutes – to get to know the room in which you will be speaking.

Many speakers walk into a room just in time to speak. As a result, they look bewildered, wonder where the microphone is, fiddle inexpertly with the volume controls, or struggle with computer set-ups in public. They may have asked for a microphone expecting a clip-on, but find one that is fixed to a high lectern, thus forcing them to remain hidden behind it. From the audience's perspective, such speakers look unprepared or uncomfortable.

For your own peace of mind and ease, it is far better to get to know the facilities in advance. No matter how busy you are, at the very worst, arrange your schedule so that you can get into the room at least five or 10 minutes before the audience arrives. If you are planning to use equipment, you need more time. Better still, check the room a few days in advance so that, if you need changes, there's time for them to be made.

Speaking of equipment: be sure you have what you need and check that it is working. If you are using a screen, have you tested one of your slides on it? Will the screen be open, or do you have to open doors, or push a button to make it appear? Where's the button? Do you need an extension cord? Will you trip over any wires that may be on the floor? Can the audience see you? Are there awkward sightlines? Do you want a lectern? Would you rather use a table instead? Does the lighting work? Where are the switches? Is the room so dark that you cannot see your notes, or so bright that the images on the screen appear indistinct?

While you are at it, check the acoustics. Are you walking on a wooden floor? Does it echo? Or do heavy curtains and thick carpets absorb sound? Do you have enough paper for your flipchart? Do you have markers? Do they have ink in them? How do you want the flipchart positioned? Can you close the door? Or are you in an open space? If so, who may be passing by? Is there another event next door that might interfere with what you are doing? Are workers hammering? Is music playing? Is a party in progress? Where are the doors? Are there phones in the room that may ring while you are speaking? Do you have water to drink? How are the seats arranged?

Look around. The more familiar you are with the room you will be using, the more comfortable you will be with the situation. You also will have anticipated and prepared for problems. If any of these potential problems are likely to interfere with your presentation, seek out the person in charge of the venue and have him or her resolve them sooner rather than later. You will be less anxious and more confident by doing so.

**See also**
Q16    Why is preparation key to communication?
Q83    What should I wear when making a presentation?

## Q83     What should I wear when making a presentation?

The answer is that it depends, but you should make a conscious decision about the image you project as a businessperson because it has an impact on the audience. You may be perceived as professional or unprofessional simply by the way you look and act. While such judgements may be fair or unfair, your image is a factor in doing business. And different fields have different looks. Bankers, accountants and stockbrokers may dress more conservatively than advertising executives, IT specialists or rock musicians. Know what is considered appropriate for your field. For some, going to work in loafers, jeans and T-shirt is absolutely acceptable; for others, it is not.

Look at yourself from top to toe. How do you appear? Do you dress appropriately for the job you have? Are you neat? Do your clothes fit? Are your collars, cuffs, and hems the right length? Anything frayed? Any buttons missing? Are your clothes clean, or is there a drop of coffee on your tie or are there ink smudges on your cuffs?

Even on 'dress down' days, are your clothes pressed? Are the heels of your shoes worn down? Are your shoes shined? While shined winged-tip shoes may not be appropriate for work on construction sites, you can still look put-together. Perhaps you are expected to wear a uniform in your job. Is it clean and pressed? Or does it look as if you threw it on a chair the night before? Are shirts or blouses tucked in? Do you need a belt? If your pants have loops, does your belt go through all of them, or just some? Does your haircut suit the occasion, or do you have a style that's more appropriate for a night on the town or that requires you to fix it? Might your clothing be considered provocative, or are you wearing patterns or combinations of colours that are startling or shocking?

Like idiosyncratic words, sounds or gestures, avoid having your clothes make a bigger statement than the messages that you are trying to share. Look at yourself and consider how you might appear to prospective client, boss or a new colleague.

**See also**

## Q84     How important is practising my presentation?

Some speakers say that they love to be spontaneous or to talk off the cuff because they feel more genuine. Often, however, they either have not taken the time or may not realise how important it is to run through a talk – a number of times. In fact, the more you practise, the more relaxed you will be. Practise your talk!

And, if possible, practise it in the room where you will be speaking. The more familiar you are with the placement of the table or chairs, the feel of the carpet, the sightlines, the acoustics, extraneous sounds, the possible interruptions, the more at ease you will be. If you cannot access the room in advance for a run-through, find another place to rehearse.

Rehearse in the office, in the bathroom, or in the car. Run through your talk a number of times, and time yourself. Practice delivering your talk aloud rather than saying it to yourself. You'll notice that the time needed for reading a speech or saying it in your head differ from speaking it out loud. Build in time for audience reaction. You may have jokes that produce laughter; so you have to wait for it to begin to subside. You may see moments where you want to pause for effect to let a powerful notion sink in or for the audience to have time to reflect on what you are saying. And you may need to slow down to change slides or let the audience take in the image. When you rehearse, build in the time the audience needs if they are watching a video or you are writing on a flipchart.

Be mindful that, if you have 15 minutes to speak, your talk should last 15 minutes, not 20. If you have 30 minutes, then your talk should last 30 minutes, not 35 or 45. And watching the time when you are part of a series of talks is even more critical. It's no different from being a patient in a doctor's surgery: if the physician takes five minutes longer with each patient, by the end of the day, the last patient may be given shorter shrift or may have to wait. In the same way, in an all-day conference, coffee breaks and lunches are usually scheduled for very specific times, and if you run long, you may force someone else to cut their speech, or you may be the one who has to spontaneously cut a speech from 45 to 20 minutes.

If you will be taking questions, have you allowed enough time for them? How many will you take? Will you be taking them from the floor, or will someone else call on the audience? Before a large audience, will you have to wait while a microphone is put in front of someone to ask their question, or do they need time to walk to a standing microphone?

The more you plan and practise, the less stressful the task becomes. You might even begin to enjoy it.

**See also**
**Q26** Why should I avoid speaking *ad lib*?
**Q85** Should I use notes during my presentation?
**Q93** How can I prepare to answer questions?

## Q85     Should I use notes during my presentation?

I always do; they are my security blanket. Some people speak extemporaneously more readily and better than others; most of us, however, cannot. However, even the most talented people may become nervous in an important situation and block, so to overcome those perfectly normal feelings, prepare notes knowing that you may never look at them. Even heads of state have tele-prompters. More than likely your talks will not be televised internationally or appear on the evening news, so you can be less formal, but having notes can make a world of difference to your nerves and to the effectiveness of your talk.

Having notes reduces anxiety and makes you appear more professional. And by notes, I mean note cards, which are actual cards, rather than sheets of paper. Have you ever seen a speaker walk to the lectern, reach into a pocket and pull out some paper and then unfold it? Is that professional-looking? While the speech that followed may have included some novel ideas, crumpled papers surely give the appearance of a rushed job. Audiences want to feel valued. They do not want to feel as if they were an afterthought.

Cards:

- Are easier to handle and less noisy than notes on sheets of paper;
- Eliminate the need for a lectern because you can move about the speaker's area more freely and with confidence;
- Enable you to gesture and to keep your head up, allowing you to maintain eye contact instead of having to look further and further down a page as you read;
- Enable you to easily reuse a talk, if all you have to do is rewrite the first or last one to tailor a talk to a particular audience.

Your note cards should hold the outline of what you are going to say. Each card holds a cue or point for you to remember. Early cards should have the first few sentences written out completely because you are more nervous at the beginning. Have them — just in case. And number your cards sequentially in case you drop them and need to put them back in order in a hurry.

If you have never used cards before, they take some practice: reading one and then putting it at the back of the pack; or moving to the next card when you didn't need to refer to a card. Once you are used to them, you can keep them in a pocket and practise at different times of the day and in different locations.

It's important to underline that these cards are your actual notes, your reminders, your outline. Your PowerPoint presentation is not your notes! Too many speakers create slews of bullets to remind themselves of what they are going to say. NO! PowerPoint is for the audience, NOT for you. Use physical notes – preferably on cards – as your own *aide memoire*.

**See also**
**Q84**    How important is practising my presentation?
**Q86**    Should I provide the audience with handouts?

## Q86    Should I provide the audience with handouts?

Providing the audience with handouts, like so much else related to presenting is a decision that you must make in preparation for a talk. You make that choice based on the purpose and complexity of your talk, and what you want the audience to remember. It is your call.

If you decide that you want the audience to have something to take away, then you need to evaluate what that 'something' should be and when they should have it.

Is the handout a reminder or is it a copy of everything you are saying? If it is a copy of your talk, did they really need to spend time listening to you? Could they have read it instead? If it is a reminder, what will they be able to recall if they don't look at it for a month? What do you need to include? What do you need to exclude to insure clarity or recall?

Sometimes a handout is particularly useful if it is a copy of a complex set of figures or graphs that is difficult for you to create on a PowerPoint slide. Perhaps you want the audience to have a copy so you can ask them to refer to it at the same time you are discussing it during your presentation.

Perhaps you are making a proposal to a potential client, and you are going over the key points in your presentation, but you want to give them the full set of recommendations in written form; in that instance, you might need a handout or a full copy of your proposal.

Remember that the timing is important. Is the handout in on a table near the entrance when they arrive? On the chairs as they sit down? Or do you distribute it during your presentation? Is it available at the door on the way out? You know that, if there is a piece of paper available on a table, people will read it. Will they read it as you are speaking? Will they read it and not hear what you are saying? Will it become a distraction? However, if you decide to time the handout to the moment that it is needed, what time will you need to distribute it? Will you do it? Will someone else help you? Do you literally have to say, "Please hold the paper until later"?

Like much of presentation, including a handout requires thought and should be built into your planning.

**See also**
**Q85**   Should I use notes during my presentation?
**Q91**   How can I help my audience retain information?

## Q87     How can I be interesting if I have given my talk before?

You have seen athletes get 'pumped up' and coaches motivating teams before a match. Before you go on stage, you need to motivate yourself. Actors do it every time they step on the stage, even if they have been in a show for years.

Think about the speakers you have seen and heard over the years. Compare those speakers who were animated about their subjects with those who seemed bored or uninterested. Which ones do you remember? What you may recall is that it is usually easier to listen to people who are enthusiastic. Why? Because they appear to believe in what they are saying and their energy is contagious. If you have to give the same talk to new hires or give virtually the same pitch to potential clients regularly, you must appear as if this is the first time you have given it and your audience consists of the most important people in the world to you – at the time.

When you want people to listen to you, the more excited you can be about your subject, the more they will hang on your words. Your tone of voice, the look on your face, your emphasis and your body language all project your enthusiasm. Do you look and sound as if you are delivering a eulogy? Do you smile? Do your eyes light up? Do you exude energy? Or do you look as if you need a transfusion?

Let your audience see that you are delighted to be speaking to them, that you care about them and about your subject. Remember that speaking is about communicating an idea or set of ideas to an audience, and for them, concentrating on a speaker for a long time is difficult. Your passion for your subject will help keep them engaged. Frankly, if you don't care about your subject, why should your audience?

### See also
**Q84**    How important is practising my presentation?
**Q88**    Why is making eye contact with the audience important?

## Q88 Why is making eye contact with the audience important?

Whether you are talking to one person, running a meeting of 20 or delivering a speech to 400, try to look at everyone in your audience. When you look directly at the audience, you appear open, frank and honest. You are indicating that you have nothing to hide.

We have all seen speakers who never lift their heads from their notes, who talk to the floor, to the ceiling, to the wall in the back over the audience's heads – anywhere but at us. Are they bored? Are they hiding something? Are they scared? We may actually begin to think more about why they aren't looking at us than about what they are saying.

No matter how nervous you are, look at your audience. They will look back at you. And try to look at everyone. Direct your gaze to the person on the far right, the left, the centre, the back, front, or around the table. Really look at people. And everyone means everyone.

Catch yourself if you find yourself talking to the person whom you believe is the most powerful in the room – the decision-maker. Decision-makers also get input from others. Catch yourself if you are talking to one person who seems to be engrossed or enjoying what you are saying. You risk alienating some members of the audience when they can see that you are not looking at them because they may think you are not valuing them as much.

Do the same when you answer a question. When you give your answer, look at everyone in the room, not just at the person who asked the question.

And when you are pointing at the screen or writing on a flipchart, do not talk to the wall or to the paper. Point or write and then turn back to the audience and speak to them. If you talk to the flipchart, you have lost eye contact and most likely your voice will not project. Write, then turn around and talk!

The other reason for looking at the audience is equally important. By watching faces and behaviour, you can gauge their reactions to what you are saying and how you are saying it. By looking at them, you can react to what you are seeing and make adjustments in the moment or for the future. Are people leaning forward trying to hear you? Are people squinting at your visuals? Are people smiling? Are they frowning? A quizzical expression on someone's face might suggest that you need to clarify your remarks by repeating what you have just said. A nodding head or heavy lids may suggest that people are tired or bored. You may have to make some sort of adjustment to your presentation to re-engage them. Perhaps you can cut part of your talk, or you can speak more quickly through the next set of points. Maybe you should change the pitch of your voice. Or stop. Or add a quick anecdote or joke. Perhaps you need to move from where you have been standing or walk closer to them or to a different part of a room. You may want to skip the next couple of slides.

In other words, maintaining eye contact is critical to you because you appear open and frank, because your audience will respond by looking back at you and because what you are seeing may suggest to you that you may need to modify your plans.

**See also**
**Q87**    How can I be interesting if I have given my talk before?

## Q89    Must I include visuals in a talk?

The simple answer is no, you don't. But it is a decision that you need to weigh. Some speakers assume that it is a given that they must use them – even when the subject matter or the time they have been allotted doesn't warrant it.

Use visuals only if they assist you in communicating what you are saying to your audience. If images serve no purpose, then don't use them.

Visuals or props may take many forms. They may not just be PowerPoint slides. They may be photographs, maps, blueprints, boxes, hand-signals or facial expressions. They may be papers you distribute. Words can be visuals too – the metaphors and similes that assist you in presenting ideas. Choose visuals that are appropriate for your message. Be sure that the images you select assist the audience in remembering your words, rather than distracting or confusing them.

To decide whether or not you need them, consider what visuals are for. They are there to help your audience understand a complex concept or as an aid to remembering a significant point or set of points. They may be used to help the audience retain your sequence of ideas or your logic. You need to weigh what you are using them for and decide whether they are appropriate for the talk you are giving. You may need only one or two – or six or seven – or none! It's OK as long as you have thought through where and how you might need them. Visuals are not a given.

While you deliberate, bear in mind that listening for a long period of time is difficult for all of us. Our minds drift away from even the most exciting speaker because we, the audience, think faster than any speaker talks. So, using only our ears to gather and retain information is less effective than using other senses too. That is one reason many of us take notes when someone speaks: most of us remember more when we both see and hear. Again, that doesn't mean that you MUST use visuals. Think about what you are going to say and make an informed decision.

Visuals frequently appear in reports or in presentations. Too often, they are hastily put together. Before preparing visuals, ask yourself why you are using them. If you are designing them because you think that they are nice to have or because everyone else seems to use them, then don't use them. If you are using visuals as prompts for yourself, then don't use them. However, if you believe that visuals clarify or reinforce your message, then by all means include them.

Remember that visuals are for the audience, not for you. Your objective is to communicate your ideas to the audience. Graphs, charts, artwork, slides and, images are all aids designed to aid the audience's understanding. Visuals are not supposed to confuse them. Therefore, like all your other communications, design your visuals with the audience in mind.

**See also**
**Q28**    What should I consider when I use images?
**Q90**    How should I introduce my visuals?
**Q92**    Should I practise with my visuals?

## Q90 How should I introduce my visuals?

Advise your audience to expect an upcoming visual. In a written report, you signal it by writing something like: "Chart 10 on page 6 indicates that the gross national product …". In other words, you direct your readers' attention to the information. Then you help them through it if need be, by suggesting that the horizontal line refers to the years and the vertical to the GNP.

When you use visuals in a talk, you should take the same approach. If it is an image projected on a wall, you might direct them by saying, "Notice the blue bar on the upper left …". In other words, you are assisting the audience so they know where they are in relationship to what they are seeing.

What you are doing is the same as tourist maps in large cities or directories in shopping malls, which mark the spot where you are standing with the words, "You are here". Your words put the audience in the picture, thus allowing them to follow you and to interpret the image with greater ease.

**See also**
**Q89**   Must I include visuals in a talk?
**Q92**   Should I practise with my visuals?

## Q91    How can I help my audience retain information?

While some of us learn better visually than orally or *vice versa*, for most of us, we retain more when we both see and hear the same phrase at the same time. If you say word for word what the audience is seeing in print on your slide, you increase the chances of them remembering. In other words, repetition both aural and visual brings home your point better.

For example, suppose you have three bullet points on the screen. Read each one exactly as it is written. Or suppose your slide is entitled "Arriving at our Mission Statement". You click on the slide and say, "Arriving at our Mission Statement" to the audience. You say exactly what is written. When the slide comes up on the screen, many speakers feel they need to be creative and use synonyms instead, so instead of saying what is written, they may say, "Our organisation created some committees to draft a statement explaining our mission". While that's a lovely sentence, it is not 'word for word' what your slide says. The audience is reading one phrase and you are saying another. So, either say nothing while the audience is reading, or repeat word for word what you wrote on the slide – giving the audience the opportunity to absorb the notion. Your objective is to have them remember your notion – in this case, your process, not your ability to use synonyms.

**See also**
**Q12**    How can I help people retain my message?
**Q86**    Should I provide the audience with handouts?

## Q92    Should I practise with my visuals?

You have undoubtedly been in an audience enough times to know all the risks when you are using technology, be it a video or a PowerPoint presentation. There is nothing worse than watching a speaker fiddling with cords, or trying to balance their laptops on a too-small lectern or having to stop because a slide didn't advance. Sometimes you have seen someone call for the IT person. And you have watched the speaker and others trying to help by looking to see which end of the cable came unplugged or clicking on the remote to find why it isn't working. Or you have been in the audience when the speaker discovers that the room is too bright, and no one knows how to darken it even after the lights have been turned out, so the images are faded. It's never pretty and is often time-wasting.

Technology has a way of creating challenges for speakers, so your objective by practising is to limit the number of problems you might be able to anticipate. So:

- Test the computer, even if it is your own laptop;
- Be sure you have a stand that will support your equipment;
- Know the location of all power switches;
- Learn how to lower or open doors to reveal screens and how to close window shades;
- Do a run-through with your slides to be sure that they are in the correct order and check for that last typo or change of date;
- Put hand-outs in the order you want to distribute them and decide where to put them;
- Arrange in advance to be shown how to use unfamiliar playback or video equipment;
- Notice what lights may reflect or dim your presentation;
- Be sure you have an extension cord – just in case;
- Check sightlines;
- Place flipcharts based on your right-handedness or left.

The more you practise with your 'props', the more you know what angles prevent eye contact, how a microphone feels or sounds, what electronic feedback may occur, and how to avoid it.

Given the layout of the room and the timing of your talk, decide how and when to distribute hand-outs. Do you have the breath, the time or the stamina to run up and down amphitheatre steps to give out material? Think about whether the audience will be reading while you are speaking.

Since you have seen things go wrong, you already know why you need to have a back-up plan. Know your materials. Have notes. Know your equipment and find time to practise.

**See also**
**Q84**    How important is practising my presentation?
**Q89**    Must I include visuals in a talk?
**Q90**    How should I introduce my visuals?

## Q93 How can I prepare to answer questions?

Answering questions is difficult and possibly more threatening to you than preparing for the talk itself. Why? You control what you are going to say, but you have no control of other people's questions – unless you have a 'plant'. You could be asked anything.

To some degree, you can prepare by reflecting on what you are saying and considering what aspects of your message might provoke questions.

Your topic may be complicated or even startling to the audience. They may not be as familiar with it as you are, so they may need clarification. Or if they have knowledge of your topic, they may disagree with your rationale. In any case, they may have questions. Presumably, when you designed your talk, you made a decision about affording the audience an opportunity to ask questions. Or whether you would take any? And, if so, for how long? Five minutes? Ten minutes? Or might you design your talk so that it is all Q&A?

So, in addition to thinking about the content of what you are saying, you prepare for questions based on your knowledge of the audience, their roles in the organisation and any of their current concerns to which your topic may relate. Assess the possibility of differing points of view on your subject, because perspectives on issues may differ from department to department and from person to person. In addition, individuals have their own agendas. As you prepare, if you work with the people to whom you are speaking, you may be able to anticipate questions that particular people with differing perspectives or agendas might ask.

On the day, you should know whether you are identifying the questioner or if someone else is going to call on them for you. You may have to repeat the question so that the entire audience hears it, which allows you a moment to think. But remember repeating a question eats into your reply time.

If you don't have an answer, offer to provide it in the future or admit that you don't know, or defer to someone in the audience who might know – IF, and only if, you don't think you are putting that individual on the spot.

And, as you well know, when people raise their hands to ask a question, and you call on them, you discover too late that they are giving a lengthy preamble and then you are forced politely to ask what their question is or whether, in fact, they have a question. Be careful too of one person asking multiple questions. Look around the room and invite others. Remember they are speaking in public, just like you, so even though they may be seated in a crowd looking at you or have a microphone handed to them, it is daunting for most of them in that moment – they have the same thoughts as you: "I hope I don't sound or look stupid", "I hope the speaker didn't say this already" or "I hope someone else didn't ask this question". How often do we say, "I hope that this isn't a stupid question" – and how often have you heard the response, "There are no stupid questions". People fear being perceived as dolts.

With a hostile audience, questioning can get tough. Don't lie. Don't blame. Assume responsibility. Stay on the point of your talk. Restate what you have said. Take the moral high ground. Avoid fighting with antagonistic members of the audience. If they persist, they, not you, will usually look bad and lose in the encounter. However, if you climb into the ring with them, you risk damaging your own credibility.

**See also**
**Q30**    How can I prepare for an emotional audience?
**Q31**    Why is it important to anticipate objections?
**Q44**    How can I prepare for difficult reactions?

## Q94    How can I stop being so nervous before a presentation?

Being nervous is normal; just don't succumb to your fear of feeling nervous. It's OK. Expect to experience stage fright.

When speaking, think of yourself as an actor performing on stage. The more you rehearse, the more you know your 'stage' or venue, the more confident you will be, and the more sure of yourself you are, the less nervous you will be. Know as much as you can about the nature and size of your audience, know your 'lines', which means having notes and rehearsing with your 'props', your visuals or equipment. Pick a comfortable and appropriate 'costume'. In essence, the more prepared you are, the more secure you should feel, because like an actor's rehearsals, practice decreases the level of uncertainty. However, expect to be nervous, particularly at the very outset, but it won't last long.

When asked, most speakers will tell you that the 'jitters' fade within a minute or two. Trust that you will be calmer.

We all experience our nervousness in different ways, so it is valuable to get to know your own brand. We have our own patterns. Does the adrenaline rush cause you to sweat or feel faint? Do your palms get wet? Do your hands shake? Does your neck turn red? Do your checks flush? Do you lose your voice? Do you suddenly find that you frequently need to clear your throat? Do your legs feel heavy, or are they weak? Do you have butterflies in your stomach? Does your heart pound? If so, is there anything you can do to control your nerves?

Here are some tips to control nervousness:
- Avoid caffeine before a talk; instead, sip room temperature water;
- Eat and eat sensibly; protein is a better choice than sugar and refined carbohydrates;
- Stand tall and take deep breaths through your nose. At the outset, when typically you are the most nervous, speak more slowly;

- Find ways of taking attention away from yourself at the beginning. Some speakers show slides or write on the flipchart so that the audience focuses on the image rather than on the speaker. Others ask the audience a question, thus putting the onus on the audience while the speaker gathers him or herself;

- Recall calming images that work for you — a lake, a clear blue sky, a beach;

- Remind yourself that you have something valuable to share with the audience and that you are in a position to make a difference!

Your nervousness will go, though it will come back the next time you speak. It is your friend, the adrenaline rush that gives you an edge and helps to make your speech a good one.

**See also**
**Q84**   How important is practising my presentation?
**Q85**   Should I use notes during my presentation?

# Q95 How should I handle team presentations?

Joint or team presentations require the same techniques that you employ when you are speaking alone, but naturally a team involves a group of people, and a group immediately suggests individuals working together but with different attitudes and strengths and weaknesses. You need to prepare and, eventually, rehearse together. The key to a team presentation is to have it look and perform like a team – not three or four people who happen to come together at a particular time or a particular day.

When you and your colleagues do your planning, decide on who is going to say what and in what order. The nature of the material might create its own logical or natural divisions, as might the individual team member's role in the research or area of expertise. So, along with issues like the length of time you have, decide on who is going to handle the introductions, if any; how you are seated; the order of the speakers; and the questions or types of questions. If you are moving from the audience to the stage, what will be the order of procession? Will you each speak for the same amount of time? Will one of you handle all the questions? Or will you each handle questions about your own specialist subject area? If you use visuals, which one of you will handle the equipment? For example, one person may advance the slides or flip the chart while another speaks. Who will distribute handouts?

During the presentation itself, the demeanour of the team members is critical. You want to help the audience stay on message. Team members who are not speaking should have their eyes glued on the person who is speaking and be actively listening to what their colleague is saying. One reason is to be sure that you can cover in case a colleague errs or technology fails. Another reason is because you are literally modelling the behaviour you want the audience to have. You want them to listen and react to what they are hearing, too. If instead of hanging on your colleagues' words, you are looking around the room or chatting with your colleague or looking relieved because your turn is over, you are distracting the audience and suggesting by your actions that what is currently being said is not as important as what you may have already said. Your demeanour should tell the audience that it is.

In essence, a team presentation is just that: an opportunity for a group to demonstrate that they work well together to achieve their goals.

**See also**
**Q84**    How important is practising my presentation?

## Q96 How can I use sound or video in my presentation?

You – and only you – should determine what will help your audience to understand your message and how you can achieve clarity in communicating. You may feel that the message and your delivery is sufficient. You may think that slides that reinforce certain key ideas with bullet points will help. You may decide that complex ideas need to be broken out. You may consider that handouts accomplish what you need.

If the goal is always to do all you can to insure that your audience grasps your concepts, then you may want to include a video or sound clip to enhance what you are doing. If a picture is worth 1,000 words, and you have a suitable image, then by all means use it. But be sure to check first whether there are any rights issues surrounding your use of a clip.

If it is OK to proceed, then determine, given the surroundings and the technology available, what is going to work. Will you simply be able to use your laptop, or must you use the AV equipment supplied? Check whether you can make the room dark enough for your audience to see any images you are projecting. If you are using audio, check whether everyone who is present can hear it clearly.

Check the equipment in advance. Will there be an IT person available? Can you talk or meet with him or her in advance?

In addition, adding a sound or video clip needs to be built into the time that you are allotted. While having multi-media may enhance what you are doing, be sure that it is part of a seamless process and doesn't detract from your overall presentation.

**See also**
**Q89** Must I include visuals in a talk?

# ACHIEVING BUSINESS COMMUNICATION EXCELLENCE

## Q97    How can I improve my ability as a communicator?

We take for granted that professional athletes, dancers and musicians practise. They develop skills, build muscles, improve fingering technique and learn how to work as a member of a team. So too should business people incorporate practice in their lives.

Become aware of your strengths and weaknesses when using the spoken or written word. Then having identified both, build on those strengths and work on diminishing your weaknesses. Increasing your awareness, followed by practice, develops your communication skills.

For example:

- When you write or receive emails, notice what is and what is not effective or appropriate?

- Have you thought about when a text is better than long note?

- Have you considered whether upper and lower case is easier to read than all bold?

- When you have to speak, pay attention to your focus. Is it on your own anxiety or on the audience?

- When you write reports and memos, are you aware of what strengthens your writing or what weakens it?

- When you appraise, interview or counsel, are you conscious of who is doing most of the talking? Are you as good a listener as you can be? Could you formulate better questions?

As you get to know yourself as a communicator, you will improve and be able to capitalise on your strong points.

Speaking in public can be frightening. Writing words for an audience is daunting. To gain confidence, rather than avoiding the situations, take the opportunities. Do it! It is easier to let someone else give the talk, to never volunteer, to find excuses for not being the one to undertake an uncomfortable situation. The more reports you have to write, the more talks you have to give, the more interviews you have to structure, the better you will become at communicating.

In addition, you may want to take courses, or work with a coach, or watch videos or read. By so doing, you will learn about your strengths and weaknesses as a communicator. Build on your strengths and diminish your weaknesses. Having done that, you will be better able to share your ideas and feelings with other people. Because you communicate with confidence, you will be more influential and more professional.

**See also**
Q98    What should I seek to learn from other speakers?
Q99    How can I develop my writing skills?
Q100   To continue to improve as a communicator, what kind of feedback should I look for?

## Q98    What should I seek to learn from other speakers?

One of the best ways to develop as a speaker is to watch other speakers make presentations. Television, as does the Internet, provides endless opportunities to see news-readers, presenters, or politicians in action.

At work, be particularly attentive to speakers at meetings. As you listen to their content, notice how they structure and sequence their thoughts, how they use examples and analogies. Pay attention to how they present themselves. Look around the room and watch the audience. Notice their reactions. See whether the speakers pay attention to the audience's reactions or if they are oblivious to them. Which speakers command attention? Why? Which ones lose the audience? What distracted them? How did a speaker keep the audience engrossed? Was it the delivery? Was it the content? Was it the words, the repetition, the humour? In other words, develop a critical eye and ear. Watch for eye contact and body language. Listen for speech patterns. True, a small meeting is different from a state of the union address, but notice techniques. Watch faces, hands and feet. Notice posture, timing and voice intonation. Evaluate the use of visuals and the visuals themselves. If an approach or strategy appeals to you, try it. Remember that imitation is the sincerest form of flattery.

But also remember that not everyone else's strategy will work for you. Because we all have different personalities, what is effective for someone else may not be right for you. While some people are comfortable throwing balls in the air or doing somersaults in the conference room, you might be uncomfortable. Don't feel badly. It's just not you.

Every time you watch someone, come away with one idea about an approach that you might use or notice a technique that you want to avoid. Next time you will smile a bit more or check your watch more often. Experiment.

**See also**

**Q97** How can I improve my ability as a communicator?

**Q100** To continue to improve as a communicator, what kind of feedback should I look for?

## Q99     How can I develop my writing skills?

The answer is by reading. One of the best ways to improve your writing is to read with a critical eye. Pay attention to the author's techniques. Are you interested in what is being said? Are you losing interest? Ask yourself why. Ask yourself why a particular report or memo causes you to lose your place or requires you to reread paragraphs or even to read it aloud in order to understand it.

Reflect on why one report is easier to read than another. You may assume that, in one instance, you were tired. But fatigue may not be the issue at all. Maybe you had difficulty making sense of the author's convoluted sentence structure. Maybe the author didn't define technical terms. Maybe the author made assumptions about what you knew about the background of the situation. Maybe there was no introduction or no structure.

Notice, too, what is visually attractive about a report and what is not user friendly. Make mental notes and incorporate effective approaches into your own written work.

And your reading may be more than reports. A columnist's choice of language, if not subject matter, may appeal to you. What's the style of your favourite authors? Why does it make them your favourite?

**See also**
**Q97**    How can I improve my ability as a communicator?
**Q100**  To continue to improve as a communicator, what kind of feedback should I look for?

## Q100 To continue to improve as a communicator, what kind of feedback should I look for?

Feedback keeps you informed about your skills and your development as a communicator. If people don't volunteer information, then ask.

Remember, don't settle for responses like "Great" or "Well done" or "Marvellous" or "Outstanding". While these are flattering words to hear, they are not adequate for your needs as a speaker or writer. You want to know exactly what you did that worked and what you did that didn't work. You may have to ask more pointed or precise questions. For example: "What did you think of the slides?", "How do you feel I handled the questioning or the questions about …?" or "What did you think about the layout of the report or the last memo that I sent?".

Train people to give you honest answers. Let them know what you expect from them because you want to replicate what you are doing well and to modify what needs enhancing. You want to apply new ideas. You want to learn from your mistakes and to repeat what works. In other words, you are developing a critical eye and ear.

Communication is ultimately about sharing ideas with each other. And developing your skills involves sharing.

Search out other people with similar interests in communicating well. Perhaps you can create a network of people in other departments who also are eager to develop their talents.

If you are anxious about a particular talk or uncomfortable with an aspect of your communication, turn to a colleague. Ask for input or for a quick review. If you do, try to be open about what they are telling you. If you trust your colleagues, understand that they want to help. They may ask you for your help as well.

Speaking and writing can make us all feel vulnerable. Few of us are comfortable being so exposed and at risk of being judged. Networking eases the loneliness. Build a network or support system to help you try out ideas or communication strategies.

**See also**

# ABOUT THE AUTHOR

Author photo: Howard Baird

**Elizabeth P Tierney**, Ph.D. is a writer, trainer, consultant and lecturer in Communications and Management. She was a school administrator in the US and taught at University College Dublin, Ireland and at Cesuga in Spain. She has trained and coached students and business people and spoken at conferences internationally. She is the author of nine other books, including three published by Oak Tree Press: **Show Time!**, **Selling Yourself**, **Dignifying Dementia** and **Quick Win Presentations**, as well as three ebooks in Oak Tree Press' NuBooks series: **Ethics in the Workplace**, **Creating an Ethical Work Environment** and **Movies for Managers**.

# ABOUT THE QUICK WIN SERIES

The **QUICK WIN** series of books, ebooks and apps is designed for the modern, busy reader, who wants to learn enough to complete the immediate task at hand, but needs to see the information in context.

Topics published to date include:

- QUICK WIN B2B SALES.
- QUICK WIN DIGITAL MARKETING.
- QUICK WIN ECONOMICS.
- QUICK WIN HR IRELAND.
- QUICK WIN LEADERSHIP.
- QUICK WIN MARKETING.
- QUICK WIN MEDIA LAW IRELAND.
- QUICK WIN PRESENTATIONS
- QUICK WIN PUBLIC RELATIONS
- QUICK WIN SAFETY MANAGEMENT
- QUICK WIN SOCIAL MEDIA MARKETING.

For more information, see **www.oaktreepress.com / www.SuccessStore.com**.

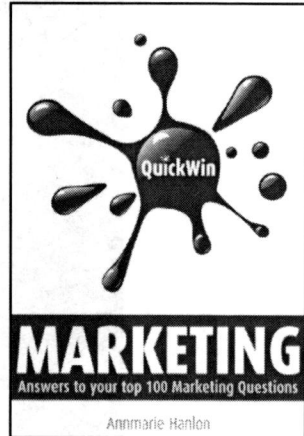